LUTHER H. HODGES,
Practical Idealist

Men of Achievement Series

LUTHER H. HODGES
Practical Idealist

by

A. G. (Pete) IVEY

Publishers

T. S. DENISON & COMPANY, INC.

Minneapolis

Dedication

To My Wife

Photo of Luther Hodges in 1917 when he was a sophomore at the
University of North Carolina in Chapel Hill.

Foreword and Acknowledgments

Young people who read this brief biography of a man whose life is guided by watchwords of punctuality, honesty and hard work will find here inspiration enough to establish a model foundation for half a dozen careers. The experiences of Luther Hodges afford a tonic that could be prescribed for boys and girls seeking a good example. But in this prescription a word of caution should be sounded. Some youths are likely to be discouraged, if exact emulation of Luther Hodges is followed. Don't take him all in one dose. He is one of the world's busiest men. He works hard. He doesn't waste time. He is punctual to the split second. He is moral, ethical, highly-disciplined, stands for no foolishness. He like to sell. He drives hard and loves to fish for relaxation. He is vigorous, stern, just, prayerful, moderate, and scrupulously fair. As his affectionate daughter says, "He is tough. Not ugly tough, but tough." Those who do resolve to read his biography with a view to possible self-application will be benefited. Others will be awed.

This book grows out of an article in the **Rotarian** of July, 1967, when former U. S. Secretary of Commerce and former Governor of North Carolina Luther H. Hodges became president of Rotary International. The writing followed interviews with Governor Hodges and members of his family and his former associates in government and in business, by research in the Southern Historical Collection in the Library of the University of North Carolina at Chapel Hill, and by information contained in Hodges' book, **Businessman in the Statehouse**, published by the University of North Carolina Press, and **The Business Conscience**, published by Prentice-Hall and Company.

Special appreciation is acknowledged for help from Edward L. Rankin Jr. of Raleigh, Paul Johnston of New York City and Chapel Hill, Thomas C. Boushall of Richmond, Va., President William Friday of the University of North Carolina, Hugh Morton of Grandfather Mountain, N. C., Prof. Albert Coates and Chancellor Emeritus Robert B. House of Chapel Hill, Dave Hodges, Mrs. Beulah Hodges Haizlip, Ethel Hodges Edwards and Otis Marlowe of Leaksville (now Eden, N. C.), Harold Whitcomb, chairman of the board of Fieldcrest Mills, Mrs. Luther H. Hodges, Luther H. Hodges Jr. of Charlotte, N. C., Betsy Hodges Bernard of Short Hills, N. J., Nancy Hodges Finlay of New Delhi, India, Jim Morton of Washington, D.C., Mrs. Louise Finlayson of Raleigh, Jack Behrman of Chapel Hill, Ralph Howland of Raleigh, Hilton West of Greensboro, and Miss Brooke Allan of the Southern Historical Collection in Chapel Hill. Invaluable were the Trip Letters which Governor Hodges has sent to his family and friends over the years, and his collected speeches when he was governor of North Carolina and Secretary of Commerce. Gov. Hodges also answered detailed questions asked of him in personal interviews.

A. G. (Pete) Ivey

Contents

Chapter One

Always on the Ball

The schoolmaster, stepping gingerly on the cross ties, led his pupils over the short railroad trestle. They followed obediently. They were taking the short cut from the Red Schoolhouse, across the main street, to the home of the man who owned the mill. It was in October of 1906.

George Deschazo, the teacher and the principal of the school, stood straight and gaunt in front of his class that morning. His face seemed redder than usual. "Mr. Mebane has invited us to his home," announced Mr. Deschazo.

B. Frank Mebane lived in a mansion. It was not far from the mill. Nor was it far from the Red Schoolhouse, nor any other place in the small town of Spray, North Carolina. The students marched from the school, across the main street, around the railroad tracks and across the trestle until they came to the entrance to the Mebane home. Two stone pillars decorated the gateway. The principal took

11

the lead, and they walked two by two up the drive-way, a graveled semi-circle in front of the big house.

Aligned in ranks, much like a troop of Boy Scouts out of uniform, they halted in the driveway and waited. Some of the older boys and girls knew what to expect. They were gleeful in anticipation. Others who had not known of the twice-a-year trip to Mr. Mebane's home wondered why they had been summoned.

B. Frank Mebane soon came out of the house. A big man, with a bigger stomach, he appeared friendly, even convivial. He seemed a trifle unctuous in his welcome. Certainly he was smooth. The thin little trickle of tobacco juice from each side of his mouth didn't detract from his role as paternal host. He wore a bright red vest.

"Boys and girls," he said, "I have a little gift for each one of you." He told them he understood and appreciated their scholarship in school. He praised their diligence in their daily lessons. Then came the main event.

Two Negro servants, dressed in white coats and dark trousers, came out of the house. Each carried a silver dish pan. On each pan was a large heap of twenty-five-cent pieces.

"A quarter for each of you," said Mr. Mebane. A servant stopped in front of each pupil, and each boy and girl reached forth a hand and took a bright silver coin from the servant.

The assembly was almost concluded. Mr. Mebane had only one final message. He said, with emphasis on each word: **"Be sure you tell your daddies what I gave you!"**

As Principal George Deschazo marched his pupils away from the mansion, the mill owner waved good-bye to them as they proceeded down the driveway, back across the trestle, and back to the Red School-house.

"Luke, what are you going to do with your quarter?" asked Munsey Hodges.

"I don't know yet," replied eight-year-old Luther Hodges.

"I'll bet he saves it," said Ethel Hodges.

Beulah Hodges said nothing. She was the young-est, six years old, and it was her very first quarter.

The four Hodges children didn't question the motive behind their windfall. "It was just a matter of delight in getting the quarter," said Luther Hodges, years later.

A child could work in the mill five hours before earning twenty-five cents. The equivalent reward for being good students and for making the trek three blocks to Mr. Mebane's home all seemed a minor miracle.

Certainly they told their fathers about it! Mr. Mebane's instruction was followed to the letter. The fathers, most of whom were employees in Mr. Me-bane's mill, had little better understanding of the reason for the man's generosity.

Election day was not far off. Mr. Mebane was not only the biggest individual mill owner in the three little towns of Leaksville, Draper and Spray. He was also the political boss of the town, and of Rockingham County.

The registration headquarters and the polling booths were in the same building with the company store where the mill workers bought their groceries and other household supplies. Luther Hodges remembers, as a boy, the lines of men in front of the company store, but longer lines on election days. Quarters given on silver trays to swarms of school children paid off on election day for Mr. Mebane when men and women of Leaksville, Spray and Draper went to the polls to vote. Political control meant economic control.

It was years afterwards, and on more mature reflection, that it dawned on Luther Hartwell Hodges that the mill owner was wielding influence and power, utilizing propaganda and offering rewards and buying votes to the end that economic and political power would continuously be controlled in that community by that one man.

Twenty years later, when Luther Hodges himself was secretary to the general manager of the mills, he helped, with others, to break the power of one-man political rule in the three towns and the county. He did this by speaking out in meetings and by helping in political campaigns. Mebane was using his political and economic power, according to many people, for personal benefit. It was apparent, too, that Mebane's interest in schools proved to be largely self-interest economically. Luther Hodges, growing up in Leaksville, championed better schools—not only for his own but for all of the boys and girls in Leaksville, Spray and Draper.

Hodges did not win quickly and immediately. He was rebuffed and criticized. Overcoming years of entrenched economic power does not often happen easily. Luther Hodges was the front man for a citizen's group who wanted better schools, and they brought suit against Mr. Mebane who had put the new Flinchum School Building on his own land. The Hodges group lost the suit. But the battle was fought also in the press and on the platform. Though losing in the first court skirmish, Luther Hodges helped to break power of the political and economic boss that had been effective since the 1890's.

Luther Hodges remembers Mr. Mebane as an intelligent and personable community leader—and boss. He was a great schemer and a marvelous salesman, and "he could have been Governor of North Carolina," said Luther Hodges.

The little boy who stood in the ranks that day in 1906 and accepted a quarter remembers the event vividly, as he remembers many other episodes of his boyhood in Spray. That same day he had awakened at 5 o'clock, before daylight. He went into the yard to a hand pumped well and brought water in the house. Earlier on the farm in Virginia his brothers and sisters had to walk down a long steep hill to a spring and carry buckets of water up the long hill. All the water was brought in by the Hodges children, nine of them. The toilet was a backhouse, or privy, outside the family's two-story home. They took their Saturday night baths in two big tubs of water.

Luther's father built the house himself. He was a carpenter—"of the jackleg variety." John James Hodges had been a tenant farmer in Virginia. But in the depression of 1898, when tobacco dropped to five cent a pound, he gave up farming.

John Hodges got three-fourths of the money for which his tobacco sold, the owner of the land one-fourth. He raised 10,000 pounds; but at five cents a pound his gross in 1898 was $375. From that amount he had also to pay for fertilizer, the upkeep of his mule and his plow. He also had to find some way to keep his family alive.

He left the log cabin in Pittsylvania County, Virginia, where his eighth child, Luther, had been born in March of that year, and he took his wife and children southward into North Carolina to the triple mill towns of Leaksville, Draper and Spray. He lived in Spray, in a house owned by the mill. With his knowledge of carpentry, he "moonlighted" and performed odd jobs. And he built his own house, for his eight children and his invalid wife.

John Hodges also built a store. He went into business for himself. At first, with his oldest children, he worked in the mill. Then he scraped together enough money to build and supply his store. With older children working in the mill and both the younger and older children working either at home or in the store, the lot of the Hodges family was certainly better than it had been in the years of tobacco farming in Virginia.

The story of the Hodges family was like that of tens of thousands of others of the past seventy-five years in the agrarian South as the people of the region moved into a mixed industrial-agricultural society. Farmers eked out a bare existence. Prices for products were uncertain from year to year. When hard times came, farmers suffered more than any other people. As farm implements became more sophisticated, as agriculture became mechanized and more could be produced per acre with fewer numbers of people, men and women moved away from the farms, as John Hodges and his family did. And, like John Hodges, they migrated only short distances, to the nearest towns where cotton mills had been established.

John Hodges was just a little more versatile and imaginative than his neighbors. And he had those eight children—all workers. The ninth was born in 1901.

The morning when Luther Hodges brought the water from the spring was a day typical of many others. His next task was to build a fire. "My first memory is of fire," said Luther Hodges. "Fire in that big fireplace." His other brothers and sisters, and his father, were at work, too, doing family chores. His mother was asleep. An invalid, she seldom left her bed. Luther Hodges remembers his mother as a kind and gentle and soft-spoken woman. A sister, Ethel Hodges, once said to her mother, "Mama, I have never seen you in a dress, or a coat, but in your gown. I'd like to see you in a beautiful robe."

Luke, for that's what Luther Hodges' brothers and sisters called him, next went to the store. There he began to sweep. It was a thorough job. Everything that the Hodges children did was painstaking. It was the way their father taught them. He insisted upon thoroughness and obedience. John Hodges was a stern man. His children respected and feared him. They performed their chores well, completely, strictly, carefully, and even cheerfully.

One of little Luke's chores was to keep the flies off the food and table during supper. "I took a branch from a tree from the yard. I'd keep it waving. How we survived as long as we did I do not know."

His sweeping job at the store finished, Luke breakfasted on warm milk, fresh from the family cow, white gravy and biscuits. Then the eight-year-old Luther Hodges picked up his books and walked to school. Ethel, 10, and Beulah, 6, walked with him. Munsey, 12, had already gone to school.

In the classroom, Luke Hodges was a good pupil. He knew his lessons. He was trained at home to avoid wastage of time, and that carried over into his school work. In Principal George Deschazo's class. Luke Hodges was quick and efficient, but sometimes his attention wandered; for he soon noted that Deschazo was not a very good teacher. As soon as classes were over, Luke was eager to get outside. For Luther Hodges was as enthusiastic about play as he was about work. He liked baseball, and tag, and pop-the-whip, and many other games he learned on the schoolground—and later on the sports he practiced at the local mill-sponsored Y.M.C.A.

The "Y" was his hangout. He trotted there at every opportunity. His recreation there was a safety-valve activity relieving the regularity of work at home, in the store, at school, and again in the store and at home after school.

After school that day, Luther returned to the store. He hitched the mare, Molly, to the grocery wagon, and then he lugged groceries to the wagon. Luther had already made the rounds of customers earlier in the week, knocking on the doors, and taking orders for weekly deliveries. Today was delivery day. He mounted to the wagon seat, grasped the reins and clucked to Molly, and they were on their way.

Hodges' store sold practically everything: groceries, meat, fresh vegetables, piece goods in large bolts of cloth, cheeses, complete suits of clothes and dresses, crackers, pickles, candies, flour, and other things ordinarily sold by a country store.

It was late afternoon when the deliveries were over. As Luther Hodges tied up the horse at the store, he said to his father, "Daddy, can I go play baseball? Some boys are playing in that lot over yonder."

John Hodges hesitated. Then he said, "All right. But be home before dark."

On the nearby sandlot, Luke Hodges immediately took his place as catcher. He was the best catcher among the boys his age. Luke aspired to be a pitcher, but his forte was behind the plate, the hot spot of baseball. He liked a good strong pitcher who could smack the ball into his mitt. Luke was a good advisor to the pitcher and to his teammates in striking play-ers out, catching foul balls and being ready at home plate for unwary sliders into the sack.

The game waxed warm and exciting, and dark-ness came before he knew it. Luther Hodges had not entirely forgotten his father's admonition to be home before dark. But he took the risk. And he lost. When he arrived home, John Hodges took the buggy whip normally applied to Molly and he beat the boy. The whip struck Luther on the legs, on the shoulders, all about his body. He yelled. He screamed because of the pain, and he yelled in the expectation that the signs of injury would result in less prolonged whip-ping.

When the punishment was done, John Hodges stepped back. He spoke to his son the cliche used by fathers in these circumstances through the ages. "Son, this hurts me more than it does you. You will thank me for this someday."

Ethel Hodges, who became Mrs. C. E. Edwards of Draper, said of her father and his severity, "Daddy really thought whipping was right and that it was the proper way to train us. In later years when Luther became successful, Daddy would say that his whippings were partly responsible."

Luther Hodges testifies: "I do have keen and harsh recollections of the discipline of my father. He was a stern person. Everybody worked in our house from the time he or she could move around. Everybody 'minded' or obeyed every instruction, regardless of how unreasonable or how untimely it seemed. By today's standards and practices, my father was cruel in corporal punishment. But we learned lessons in good behavior which certainly helped us in later life."

If John Hodges had been living when Luther H. Hodges became Governor of North Carolina and Secretary of Commerce in the Cabinet of John F. Kennedy and Lyndon B. Johnson, it is entirely likely, said Luther's sister, that the father would give equal credit to Molly's old buggy whip, as well as to Luther Hodges' ambition, determination and imagination.

When John Hodges had gone, after the whipping, Lessie and Ola Hodges rushed to Luther's side. They led the weeping boy to their room. They washed his cuts and bruises with warm water. They painted him with iodine. They brought him supper. They soothed their brother's feelings with soft words. They took him to his room and put him to bed. Luther Hodges said his prayers, and slept soundly until 5 o'clock the next morning.

Christmas was not much different from other days in the Hodges' household. "My father, who was head of the house in every respect, thought very little about Santa Claus," said Luther Hodges. There were no presents and no holiday spirit; no tree; nor any exchange of gifts. "Of course, we had no money, but more than that we didn't have the tradition like some folks," he added. But it was not a total loss. On Christmas Eve, John Hodges would bring something from his store. It was a twenty-pound sack of oranges and nuts. The oranges and nuts were passed out to the nine children on Christmas morning. "I can still remember peeling an orange with such great de-light," said Luther. "My once-a-year orange was made to last for days and days. I kept the peelings and let them dry so that I could continue to enjoy the precious things."

Luther Hodges was the kind of boy people pre-dicted would make good in the world. His sisters and brothers noticed something special and different about Luther and they were proud of him. His school teachers observed his industry, and they encouraged him. He was industrious, affable, humble, and seemed to be equipped with a driving energy and an outlook mature for his age. Ambition and deter-mination seemed to be hallmarks of his character. "Luther was going to be something and somebody," said Ethel Hodges Edwards. "Whatever he did, he did well. He was not an extremist. He was just always on the ball."

That trait of being willing to work hard and aspire to a higher plateau in life was shared by other members of the family who grasped opportunities when they came their way. "I think it was a kind of pride," said Beulah Hodges, later Beulah Haizlip of Leaksville. "It was just a feeling that we intended to do our part to accomplish worthwhile things, and to be respectable."

The Hodges brothers and sisters had diverse in-terests, but "perfectly wonderful relationships," Luther Hodges declares. "I do not recall any incident where there was any real argument or disagreement among or between the brothers and sisters. It may be that our father's stern treatment of us pulled us closer together."

The Hodges' were a religious family. They attended the Methodist Church. John Hodges was often called upon to pray in church. "He would get up from the bench and halfway kneel in the aisle as he prayed aloud," said Ethel. In the home, family Bible reading and prayers were a regular program, each of the children being called upon to pray. John Hodges talked to God in a conversational tone.

On Sundays, according to the custom of the community, they all went to Sunday School and church. Luther was invariably well prepared in his Sunday School lessons. He was only too ready to recite when his turn came. As he sat there and heard others speak, he thought to himself, "I wonder what I would say if I were in front of the class—if I would say it the same way, or if I could say it better?"

Luther Hodges made a mental, but unspoken, promise to himself: to always be prepared to take someone else's place if that person should falter. "I wanted to be so apt and ready that I could instantly assume that other person's place, if he should die in his tracks, or otherwise have to give up," said Luther Hodges.

That motto of the Boy Scouts, learned long before Luther Hodges became a Boy Scout, was early ingrained, and remained with him through the years.

Being prepared, being punctual and **conserving his time** are three qualities Luther Hodges developed in his own personality from his earliest years.

When he became an executive of Fieldcrest Mills and of the whole Marshall Field and Co. manufacturing complex, and when he became Governor of North Carolina and Secretary of Commerce, a foremost consideration in his daily regimen was: **Be on time.** When he finds that despite all precautions he must be late for an appointment, he tries to call ahead and notify people why he cannot be there at the appointed minute, and he sets another time for the engagement.

His sisters recollect another time when he was late coming home, after gymnasium fun at the Y.M.C.A. It was after dark, and there were no streetlights to guide the way. John Hodges had warned Luther to be home before dark. But time again had sped away. As he crept through the darkness in front of the house, Luther Hodges had not reckoned on an obstacle in the street in front of his home. It was the family cow. In the pitch blackness he stumbled and sprawled over the cow. The animal, disturbed, rose to her feet. The boy was thrust upward on the cow's back. Luther yelled loudly, waking up the household and bringing out again, alas, the buggy whip.

Although Luther Hodges does not favor or practice corporal punishment, he does not differ with his father's view on the influence Molly's buggy-whip had on his character. "It could be," he said, "that I owe my punctuality to those early days when I was taught rather roughly to be on time." Anyhow, the habit has stuck with him.

Luke received no pay for his chores at home and for his work in the store. Those were obligations deriving from membership in the family. What money he made he obtained from extra employment, chiefly by selling newspapers. He sold **Grit,** an all-purpose publication that came from Pennsylvania. He also sold the **Saturday Evening Post.**

Beulah Hodges Haizlip remembers: "Luther used to tease me, as brothers do tease younger sisters. When I cried he would become upset and a little angry because I had made a fuss. Then he would make up. He would take me for a trip on his bicycle which was a $3.00 second-hand bike. I'd ride with him on the handle bars."

The sisters occasionally accompanied Luther on his grocery rounds, helping to deliver the merchandise from house to house. Once, when they were not along, Luke was late coming home. But it was not a whipping offense this time. Molly returned without him. She drove up in front of the house, without the boy driver.

Soon Luther arrived home, his clothing torn and disheveled. In going down a hill the shaft had struck the horse on the rump, and she became frightened and ran away. Luther was thrown from the wagon into a ditch.

Beulah and Ethel recall another injury suffered by Luther that carried more of a permanent scar. "We liked to jump from the upper story of the barn to a pile of hay below," said Beulah. "One day Luther jumped, but didn't get clear of the side of the barn. His head hit on a ten-penny nail, and gashed his forehead. We took him in the house. He was bleeding like a stuck pig."

No doctor attended him. The sisters took care of it. "I believe we used three kinds of medicine on him," said Ethel. "Iodine, kerosene and soot." Luther Hodges bears the mark of the ten-penny nail to this day.

In a day and under circumstances that seem harsh by comparison with mid-20th-Century times, Luther Hodges seemed undismayed by the rigors of his boyhood. When he ran into trouble, he surmounted it. When he found he couldn't do a job one way, he tried another. He was, in temperament, undiscouraged. When blocks were put in his path, he climbed over them. He didn't react antagonistically to rebuffs. He tried again and again. "Disappointments didn't faze him," said Beulah. "He took it on the chin, and came back again. When he was working hardest, he was jolly. Luke was determined to succeed in everything he did."

His father was a native of Franklin County, Virginia, and he moved with his wife, Lovicia Gammon Hodges, several times and to half a dozen farms, before he finally turned his back on farming. John Hodges' father was a Confederate soldier, and his ancestors had come to Virginia from England. It was a trademark of the Hodges family that has come to be called in these days "togetherness." John Hodges had a brother, and they farmed near one another whenever they migrated from farm to farm in Virginia. When John Hodges came to Leaksville to work in the mills, his brother moved, too.

The adversity experienced by the Hodges, their habit of hard work, their strict way of life, and the illness of Lovicia Gammon Hodges, all visited upon John Hodges a greater sense of anxiety and responsibility for his nine children and their upbringing than the ordinary man of poor prospects encounters. His stern discipline matched his devout outlook on training, and it is apparent he obeyed the Biblical counsel that "to spare the rod is to spoil the child." Under such discipline, a boy grew up, aided undoubtedly by contact with school and books, games and Y.M.C.A., and the closeness of family association that thrived between the brothers and sisters. Luther Hodges, as his life shows, gives extra meaning to the old saying, "Sweet are the uses of adversity."

Out of such association there emerged a boy with drive, determination, ambition, a sense of wanting to elevate himself in life. He aspired, for a time, to attain another goal: to become a missionary. This was probably based on his church training and the stories of achievements of missionaries in far-off lands. Luther Hartwell Hodges developed early in life a sense of mission.

"Let Luther Do It" was the slogan. Here is Luther Hodges "about to do it" as a young executive secretary to the manager half a day and a laborer in the mill the other half a day. About 1920.

Chapter Two

Don't Be Beholden to Anybody

"Luke, you'll have to keep the store," said John Hodges.

It was only for a few minutes. John Hodges was headed for the barber shop.

Luther Hodges was only ten years old. He had worked in his father's store for several years, sweeping, hauling and even selling. But this was the first time he had been left alone, and responsible.

He prided himself on being prepared, ready to take someone's place. He was delighted. He was confident. He was determined to make good with this temporary trust.

He walked down behind the grocery counter. His eyes scanned the patent medicines on the rack. He hustled to the other side of the store and looked at the entrancing bolt goods and the men's suits, shoes and shirts that had just come in from the Baltimore Bargain House. He looked into the cracker barrel. He placed a knife beside the large cake of cheese. He set a jug on a table beside the big barrel

of Puerto Rican molasses, ready to fill the jug for
any customer.

As Luther inspected the produce, he heard someone coming in the front door. He detected a lurching
sound. The ten-year-old boy saw the customer,
slightly unsteady on his feet. But it **was** a customer
and Luther said, "What can I do for you, sir?"

The man looked quizzically at the boy behind the
counter. He looked all around the store. "Are you in
charge?" he asked.

"Yes, sir," said Luther Hodges.

"Well, I'd like some Jamaica Ginger," said the
customer.

"How much?" asked Luke.

"How much have you got?" asked the man.

Luther counted the bottles on the shelf. He had
18 bottles of the stuff. He relayed the information
to the man.

"I'll take all of it," the man said.

Luther considered himself indeed in luck. A man
buying out the entire supply of ginger. He took all
the 18 bottles off the shelf and packed them into a
pasteboard box.

"Charge it," said the man. He weaved his way
out of the store, laden with a medicine and refresh-
ment that only a few years later, in 1913, was pro-
hibited for sale by North Carolina law because of its
alcoholic content.

When John Hodges returned, his son proudly showed him the sale he had completed, even though on credit.

Luther didn't get a licking, because John Hodges was as amused as he was amazed.

"You've sold my entire stock of Jamaica Ginger to the town drunk," he said.

One hundred yards from the Hodges store was a slaughterhouse, also owned by John Hodges. He killed cows, calves and hogs. Then he skinned them. The Hodges boys carried the quarter of beef, or more, on their backs, or in a wagon, to a lean-to at the rear of the market. The meat was sold to the customers, still warm. There was no refrigeration.

The first step in butchering a cow was to knock it in the head. "My father, who was fairly strong," said Luther, "could kill a cow with a big sledge hammer." Luther looked forward to the day when he would be able to put a cow out of its misery with one blow. One day he tried it. He aimed a blow at a good-sized calf. "The blow made very little impression," said Luther Hodges, "from the butchering standpoint, but enough to cause the calf to seek to defend himself. The calf started after me, and I ran."

At the Y.M.C.A. Luther Hodges was so active that the Secretary of the "Y" put him on a "Governing Board" of boys. He took these duties seriously and worked in concert with the adult board of the "Y," which actually supervised the activities. It was the kind of responsibility he liked.

Luther said, "I'm afraid my extra activities, which I could participate in by stealing moments from my work and my studies, caused my studies to suffer. I never was a real scholar."

When he was twelve years old, Luther Hodges one day came close to being a permanent drop-out from school. It was in George Deschazo's class, the same lean, red-faced teacher who had marched the Red Schoolhouse children to the home of mill-owner B. Frank Mebane for the twenty-five-cent pieces.

Deschazo asked Luther Hodges a question. Luke not only didn't answer right away (he seemed to be absorbed in far-away thoughts) but when he did reply the answer didn't suit his teacher. Irked, Deschazo struck the boy across the face with the book.

Luther immediately wanted to drop out of school, and he told his father so. It was not the first time Luther had felt Deschazo's antagonism. The father agreed, but only temporarily. "The new school will be built next year," he said. "You can quit school now and go to work for awhile, if you go back to school next year."

Luther had gotten along with his teachers and remembered with love and affection Miss Katie Stocks and Miss Elizabeth Taylor. He still liked school and made up his mind that the absence from classes because of Deschazo would not be for long.

Luther took a job in the mill. He was an office boy, one of three working for the Carolina Cotton and Woolen Mills, a predecessor of Marshall Field and Company's Fieldcrest Millls. Fieldcrest was a successor to several mills owned by B. Frank Mebane that had gone into bankruptcy. Marshall Field and Co. bid for the mills at an auction.

C. P. Wall was the man who hired Luther Hodges as office boy. "He was a very good man, a slight man with an authoritative manner," said Hodges. "He brooked no foolishness."

Mr. Wall became exasperated with his office boys on sufficient provocation. Duties consisted of running errands, carrying documents through the mills, delivering mail to the post office, operating a letter press for filing records, and other chores. Luther's pay was five cents an hour. He worked ten hours a day, six days a week, totaling sixty hours. The three dollars a week looked good to the twelve-year-old boy.

One time, in sixty days of competition for excellence between the three boys, Luther Hodges won a watch, given to him by the mill management.

It was not all drudgery. The boys often had time on their hands. They crawled into the furnace room, usually a forbidden place. "We had fights pretty regularly," Hodges remembers. He became proficient in rough and tumble wrestling, and he could hit a very good punch with his fists. On their way to the post office with the mill's mail, the office boys fell into the habit of annoying Charlie Wong, who operated a Chinese Laundry of the same name. This meant, primarily, calling insults like:

Chink, Chink, Chinaman, ain't no good;

Chink, Chink, Chinaman, stole some wood.

One day Charlie Wong taught them a lesson. He greeted them with smiles as they passed his laundry. Not only that, but he invited them inside to show them "something special." On a table, the laundry-man had a small, dressy, exotic-appearing decanter. "Smell this," said Charlie Wong. Luther Hodges bent over the decanter and took a whiff. The chemical ingredients inside must have been something like tear gas. It burned his eyes. He choked up. There was no lasting harm. Charlie Wong got a tremendous kick out of it. There was a notable cessation of insults hurled at Charlie Wong by Luther Hodges and his two office-boy associates.

After sixteen months as office boy, Luther Hodges returned to school. Meanwhile, however, he had reached the age of thirteen. One day he suffered a shock. His mother, an invalid in all of his remembrance, died. The frail, gentle woman who loved him was gone.

There was no spectacular disease from which Lovicia Gammon Hodges suffered. "She just wore out," thinks her daughter Ethel. "It was a case of having too many children in a short period of time, in an age when there wasn't enough health and medical knowledge to know what to do about it." If medical care had been in the early part of the century what it is today, Lovicia Hodges would have been a strong and active woman and long-lived, the children believe. As it was she was afflicted by a series of debilitating ailments that finally proved fatal.

Luther Hodges at 15, a student in Leaksville High School (1913).

In high school Luther Hodges renewed his interest in books with a resurgence of enthusiasm that delighted his teachers. He was good in Latin and in Greek. The superintendent of the high school, the Rev. Price Henderson Gwynn was the most avid of prophets about what young Luther Hodges might be able to accomplish. Mr. Gwynn's words of praise caused Luther Hodges to increase his efforts. He came to recognize that his toils were indeed appreciated and that something might come of his labors after all.

It was the Rev. Mr. Gwynn who first suggested, "You ought to prepare yourself for college. I think you will be able to qualify to enter the University of North Carolina. Keep at it, and you will go successfully through college in Chapel Hill."

But that was not the ultimate of Mr. Gwynn's forecasts. Noting Luther's speaking abilities, his quickness of mind, his drive, and his attention to detail, as well as his independence, Price Gwynn said, "Luther Hodges will someday be Governor of North Carolina."

In the summertime, Luther returned to work in the mill. He learned to operate the looms. He was a weaver and a good man with a repair kit.

One day his foreman, Nelson McBride, a genial and friendly man, commended Luther for his work. "Why don't you stay right here in the mill?" he said to the boy. "You have a great future here."

Luther thanked him, and he added, "But I want to go to college," he said. "I intend to go to the university in Chapel Hill."

"But it takes a lot of money to go to college," said McBride. "You don't have any money. But you're a bright young fellow. I'd guess that in another couple of years you won't be making just fifteen cents an hour. I'll guarantee that if you do your job well, as you're doing now, that in two more years you'll be making twenty-five cents an hour!"

"Twenty-five cents an hour!" That was big talk. But Luther and McBride knew it was no exaggeration. However, Luther Hodges had even greater visions than that.

He could see in himself, in his future, a man who lived by principles, by the Golden Rule, by the Ten Commandments, by hard work, by saving, by being punctual, by being ready to do the dirty work, and by volunteering for the onerous tasks.

"Luther had another idea," said Buelah, his sister. "He didn't want to be beholden to anybody. He frequently used that word — 'beholden.' He wanted to be independent, to do things for himself."

Most of the Hodges children had left home by around 1913 and 1914. The eldest, Dave Hodges, fourteen years older than Luther, had been working in the mill for years. Munsey Hodges was married at the age of sixteen, and left home. Blanche Hodges married and lived in Roanoke, Virginia, where her husband worked for the Norfolk and Western Railroad. Three other sisters were married and lived in Leaksville, or Spray or Draper. Luther Hodges, with his immediately older sister, Ethel, and Beulah, the youngest and pet of the family, remained at home.

When Luther Hodges was fourteen, his father remarried. John Hodges returned to his old home in Franklin County, Virginia, and brought back to Leaksville as his wife an acquaintance he had known in his younger days. "Miss Mary," as the Hodges children called her, was a good woman and devoted to John Hodges. But the presence of a stepmother upset the sense of security of the children who remained in the home.

Luther Hodges stayed at home only a short time after the wedding. He went to live with a sister, Mrs. Annie Hopper, who lived in town. Luther made another decision. He would drop out of school again, but not for long, only long enough to earn enough money to start his way in Chapel Hill. He had heard about campus jobs, and scholarships and methods whereby a student might work his own way, and he was determined to make the try. But first he had to accumulate a tiny nest egg, something to pay for a foothold in education in Chapel Hill.

His sister, Blanche Crews of Roanoke, Virginia, told him the welcome mat was out. Luther could live in their home and get a job, perhaps on the railroad.

He packed his belongings, including a blue serge suit that was the only suit he owned, and took a train for Roanoke, Virginia.

"I found odds and ends of jobs in Roanoke," Luther Hodges said. "These paid only ten to twenty cents an hour, but even that was a lot of money." One of the toughest jobs he had was a brickmason's helper. He carried loads of brick on his shoulder up ladders to the bricklayers.

One evening Blanche Crews met Luther at the door when he came home. She held in her hands that day's edition of **The Roanoke Times.** The Union News Company was advertising for a news butcher to sell merchandise on passenger trains.

Luther Hodges presented himself at the Union News Company early the next morning. A little fat man looked him over. "You look likely," the roly-poly man said jovially. He asked Luther a few questions, and seemed satisfied with the answers. But he was skeptical of one thing. "You say you don't have but a dollar and twenty-five cents," he told young Hodges. "How are you going to buy the uniform?" He added, "We also require cash security." The "uniform" consisted of a blue coat with bright brass buttons and a cap. Luther looked downhearted. But then he suddenly said, "How about this double-breasted blue coat I'm wearing? I can reverse it and use the brass buttons when I am working. I can get my sister to sew the buttons on the coat."

The man looked at Luther Hodges with cautious admiration. Then Luther clinched it. "If you'll sell me the buttons for 15 cents, I'll be in uniform by tomorrow," he said.

The man waived the cash security of $30 for his stock of goods. The cap cost $1. That is how Luther Hodges got the job. Half a century later, the Advertising Council of America featured United States Secretary of Commerce Luther H. Hodges in an advertisement displaying the value of newspaper classified ads.

"Peanuts! Popcorn! Chewing gum! Crackerjack! Ice cold pop! Newspapers and magazines" These were the items and that was the list of merchandise that Luther Hodges, the news butcher, hawked down the aisles of passenger trains on the Norfolk and Western branch line from Roanoke, Virginia, to Winston-Salem, North Carolina.

After two months, Luther was transferred to the main line between Roanoke and Norfolk. However, Luther traveled eastward on "Number 3" only as far as Suffolk, Virginia. Then he caught "Number 4" back to Roanoke. Luther enjoyed the run, but he regretted that he didn't get to go all the way into Norfolk. It became something of a minor ambition to go there. He'd never seen the ocean. He wanted to look at it.

"One day it happened," Luther Hodges said. "For some reason Number 4 was late. I was authorized to go on into Norfolk and spend the night and come back the next morning. I was thrilled. I had good sales going down to Norfolk. I must have had fifteen or twenty dollars in my pocket. I had no friends or acquaintances in Norfolk. I just knew that I wanted to see the ocean. I saw it; thrilled at it."

His next move was to find a place to stay for the night. "I found a flophouse, for twenty-five cents, and was able to spend the night lying on a pallet on the floor. Eight or nine other people were in the place. Most of them were tough-looking men."

Luther Hodges lay down with his money clutched in his hands so that he would waken immediately if anyone touched him. "No one bothered me," he reported. "I got up ready to make the return trip. It was a great experience."

In a few months Luther Hodges had saved enough to justify a return to Leaksville. But that was only a way station this time. His long-range objective was to complete high school—it would take only another five months—and then enroll in the University of North Carolina, even though he would be "conditioned" on three subjects.

When he returned to Leaksville, he went back to his father's home and his stepmother. He told his father of his ambition. "I won't stand in your way," his father said. "But I can't help you. None of your brothers and sisters have gone to college. I haven't helped any of them. If you go, you will have to go on your own."

That was all right with Luther Hodges. He talked with the Rev. Price Gwynn and others in Leaksville and his resolve was firm. He pitched into his studies with dedication. He continued his work in Leaksville at the Y.M.C.A. and at the Methodist Church. He played soccer and basketball. He had a yearning to win—to win at anything and everything he did. Such ambition caused a bit of trouble one day. A big boy of the high school, whose name was Burgess, challenged Luther to a fight. Luther knew he was on his mettle because Burgess had beaten all other boys in the school who stood up to him. But it was only a matter of a few seconds before Luke Hodges had his adversary on his back. Luke was pronounced winner. "Burgess and I were good friends for the years afterward," said Hodges.

Luther Hodges remembers his route to Chapel Hill in September of 1915. He took the Danville & Western (nicknamed the Dick and Willy) train from Spray to Danville, Virginia, and changed to the main line of the Southern Railway, running into Greensboro, North Carolina. Then he took the branch line towards Durham, changing at University Station in Orange County. The next trip was into Carrboro, a mile from the campus of the University of North Carolina in Chapel Hill.

He paid twenty-five cents to have his trunk hauled by wagon to Carr Dormitory on the campus and he walked!

When he reached his room, Luther Hodges emptied his pockets and counted all the money he had in the world—the resources on which he could begin four years in the University. The total was sixty-two dollars and fifty cents.

The freshman Luther Hodges had achieved one of the first major ambitions of his life. He was now in Chapel Hill, and headed for goals that even the Rev. Price Gwynn had not anticipated.

Chapter Three

Freshman at Chapel Hill

It was the first day of classes. Luther woke up early. No one was stirring, except for a squirrel frightened up the trunk of a giant oak. Luther drank from a bucket at the Old Well. To his right was Old East, the "first" building erected at a state university in the United States. To his left was Old West. Directly ahead were well-spaced trees, a garden-like forest, carefully tended. The ground was smooth and sloping, a green landscape through which gravel pathways coiled—bordered with shrubbery. The boy knew it took a lot of work to keep up that kind of landscape. More than that, it had required time— 122 years of devoted gardening, pruning, and protecting. Behind him a bell began to ring. He turned and looked at Old South Building. All three places had the modifier "old" in front of their names—Old East, Old West, Old South, Old Well. But Gerrard looked just as old, and so did the YMCA, Memorial Hall, Person Hall, and the Library. "I suppose the freshmen are the only new things here today," thought Luther.

The Reverend Price Gwynn had told him that Chapel Hill was venerable, the oldest state university in the United States. Just last night a senior, helping to acclimate freshmen into the folklore of Chapel Hill, told how a party of men rode through these woods looking for a likely place to build the University of North Carolina. They stopped beneath the shade of a big poplar tree. "That tree is still there," he said. "It's our local shrine. We call it the Davie Poplar, named for General William Richardson Davie." Twenty yards from that tree was the place where they built Old East. "Cornerstone laid October twelfth, seventeen hundred and ninety-three," said the senior profoundly. The freshmen looked respectfully at Old East, a brown, ivy-covered, three-story structure used as a dormitory.

Amid these signs of antiquity, Luther looked hopefully for something new. In mathematics class that morning he watched the reaction of his classmates when the instructor called the roll. He played a game of listening, matching and remembering names and faces, as many as he could without turning his head and staring. The teacher pronounced the names: "Abernethy, Barden, Boren, Bynum, Chatham, Cobb, Dortch, Eaton." Luther Hodges answered to his own. The instructor concluded with "Rondthaler, Schenck, Vogler, West, Wimberly."

President Edward Kidder Graham stood at the podium before 1,000 students assembled in the University auditorium. Most of the 98 faculty members were present and waiting for his words, for this was the first speech to be made by the new President of the University of North Carolina since his inaugural of the previous spring. Luther sized him up as a man in his middle thirties, a tall, scholarly-looking gentleman, not frail, but not robust.

Suddenly Luther Hodges realized that President Graham was speaking directly to him. The President spoke to the students and faculty, particularly to the freshmen, on "The College and Human Need."

"I ask you two questions," Graham said. "Upon what does the greatness of the University depend? Upon what does your success here and your own greatness as a university student depend?" Luther Hodges had already been thinking about both questions, and now the President of the University was going to answer them. He listened intently. President Graham spoke easily and fluently:

> The greatness of a college depends upon its ability to satisfy the supreme human need of the people and the time it serves. The great college is the college that supplies the civilization it serves with a program of guidance—a way out of the difficulties through which the people are trying to find their way, and equips its students to be representative men in the era in which they live.

> Your own success here and your greatness as a college student depend on your ability to train yourself through your quiet days of study here in those qualities which will be demanded of the representative man in the world in which you are preparing to take your place.

Yes, this seemed reasonable to Luther Hodges. He was indeed seeking some kind of guidance. He wanted to extricate himself from difficulties—that was certain. These difficulties were grounded in the poverty he had experienced in Leaksville, and he wanted that freedom to achieve the greatness that Edward Kidder Graham was talking about. Luther wanted success, and he waited to hear the words that would provide him a new set of rules, or a re-fabrication of old rules. He was willing to study and to be trained. He perked up as Graham said he was going to consider four qualities essential as pre-requisites:

First: No student is truly trained unless he has learned to do pleasantly, and promptly, and with clean-cut accuracy every task he has obli-gated himself to do. Decisive and purposeful performance of every duty is a fundamental rule of success in life that no man has the right to train himself away from in college.

Second: No student is truly trained unless, in addition to getting this mastery of the tools of life that comes through the discipline of routine tasks, he puts into his work his own per-sonal curiosities and opens his faculties to a live-ly and original interest in his work which leads him to test for himself what he has been told.

Third: No student has been truly trained unless in addition to learning to do a workman-like job, and cultivating a lively spirit of in-sistent inquiry, he also gets from his contact with the master spirits of the race those quali-ties of taste and behavior and standards of judg-ment that consititute a true gentleman.

Fourth: In addition to these individual in-terests, no student is truly trained unless he realizes that he does not live to himself alone, but is a part of an organic community life that is the source of most of the privileges he enjoys.

Perhaps of all the hundreds of students in that hall, few were more ambitious than Luther Hodges in a determination to do the work President Graham was recommending; to do the routine tasks pleasantly and with clean-cut accuracy. Luther was willing and eager to acquire the training; he was already highly disciplined. He wasn't sure about his tastes and behavior and standards of judgment. But he was willing to find out all he could about them.

Two days later President Graham made another speech and Luther listened raptly. These key works inspired him as much as any sermon he had ever heard:

> The adventure of discovering and liberating one's mind, far from being a dull and dreary performance, is the most thrilling of all youthful adventures. There is no question of self-punishment or external discipline, only the freedom of becoming one's own master instead of a slave to the tyranny of one's low and cheap desires. To come into this insight is to see this organized discovery of the mind that we call education not as learning, but as a love of knowledge, not as a matter of being industrious, but of loving industry, not as a matter of beginning a good start toward success, but of enabling us to keep growing, and so to lay hold on the eternal spring of life.

Not only the choice of words and the ideas they expressed seized the students of 1915, but Graham himself was impressive. There was a glow about him,

an earnest but easy vitality. His seriousness of purpose, his spiritual quality, his stability of character,
the dignity of his personality, his force and power
and the leadership that seemed to come from a sense
of service and religious faith—these were appealing,
especially to Luther Hodges who had already been
brought a part of the way along a path to higher
education.

Chapel services were held daily. It was compul-
sory for freshmen and sophomores. The speaker, day
in and day out, with rare exceptions was President
Graham. Everyday he had something new and fresh
to say. Although juniors and seniors were not obligated to attend chapel, they came to hear Dr.
Graham. They didn't want to miss anything. Graham
had a knack of taking everyday events, some topic
of the day, and turning it into a moral lesson for all
time. Before he became president he had taught
English and journalism. He was ahead of his time as
a public relations man. He was practical as well as
theoretical, and public service was a part of his
fabric.

Luther Hodges was to find out that President
Graham wanted to pass along to students, including
freshmen, a degree of independence, freedom, responsibility and authority. Luther liked the concept
of student self-government which President Graham
deemed a central part of the life on the Carolina
campus. This was democracy as Luther had thought
it should be. Here in Chapel Hill was Luther's chance
to see democratic representation in action. Upper
classmen had said this was a cloistered, isolated place

where a working model of self-government could be tried—and everyone had a part in it, as much as he pleased and to the extent of his abilities.

The University, President Graham and the student government were all combined with a certain new spirit of seriousness. This sober facade was heavy. There was an overtone of war talk. When war was declared in Europe in 1914, Luther Hodges was only dimly aware of its significance to America. He was more immediately concerned with selling "Extras" that day as he hawked the newspapers. But students at Chapel Hill became affected by the war psychology. Increasingly they became aware that most of them would go into service sooner or later. Faculty members saw in their classes a more serious determination to get the most out of studies. The freshmen noticed another thing. There was an almost complete absence of hazing. Just three years before a student had been killed because of it. Now, in 1915, the senior class was the students who had seen the high mark of hazing in the University, and they were determined not to practice it, nor see it done by others on the University campus. This spirit of mutual respect and mature intent suited Luther Hodges. He studied. He labored to make up the academic deficiencies that he had brought to Chapel Hill from Leaksville High School.

The football season was starting. Luther didn't go out for the freshman team. He was waiting for basketball in the winter and baseball in the spring. First he planned to get a self-help job. His $62.50 was almost gone. But Luther played football among his dormitory mates in Carr Building. He learned yells and songs that would encourage the team.

The football season began in a new stadium. It was a gift to the University of North Carolina by one of its alumni successful in chemistry and in operating drug stores, but particularly in mixing, patenting and popularizing a headache powder known as Bromo Seltzer. Colonel Isaac Emerson of Baltimore gave the money to build Emerson Stadium in Chapel Hill. After leaving Durham, North Carolina, Emerson made millions on his pick-me-up discovery.

Late in September while crossing the campus Luther was hailed by an older student.

"You're Luther Hodges from Leaksville, aren't you?" he asked. "I'm Jim Price. My home is in Rockingham County, too. I came here from Madison." Madison was only a few miles south of Leaksville. James Valentine Price was studying to be a doctor. The University at that time had a two-year medical school. "How are you getting along?" asked Price.

Luther said he was doing all right in his studies. "But I do have one problem," he said.

"What's that?" asked Jim Price.

"Eating," said Luther. "I'm eating right now, but I don't know how long I will last. I need a job. I have to pay my way. I've spent about all that I brought with me from Leaksville, and there is no more."

Price had the solution. "A bunch of us medical students are wanting to go to Swain Hall," he said.

"I understand that if ten of us get together, and if we can get someone who wants the job of waiting on our table, he can get his board free. How would you like to do that?"

Luther grasped the opportunity. Swain Hall was the student commons, the place where the large majority of students swarmed for their three meals a day. He was the waiter for the ten medical students. They came into the dining hall wearing their white coats. "I can still smell the odor they brought from the medical laboratories," Luther Hodges said years afterwards. "I can still recall that there were some rather ribald stories and jokes. But I ate and ate well for a student who was not accustomed to much."

Besides being a waiter, he also put in extra time in the Swain Hall kitchen, helping with dishes. But in the division of duties between washing and wiping dishes, he finally settled for the specialty of wiping.

A fellow waiter and dish wiper in the big kitchen was Leary Adams who was to become a newspaperman. Almost forty years later when Hodges became governor of North Carolina, Leary Adams remembered those Swain Hall days:

The new governor is the kind of man you never forget.

When we were working together in old Swain Hall kitchen at the University of North Carolina in Chapel Hill, I considered him the fastest dish wiper I have ever seen—that is, the fastest with the exception of me.

When I realized (years later) that young Hodges had done well as an industrial leader I felt a tremendous lift. He was the kind of young man you always hoped and believed would succeed. He was always moving forward, but not selfishly. He was interested in everybody around him and in all their minor successes and aspirations—for after all, big successes are built on the solid rock of minor ones.

As I remember him, he was always seeing the possibilities in other people he knew and pointing to their achievements on the campus and on the athletic field. He had an accurate and true memory of facts and incidents, the instinct and desire to make something constructive out of them.

It seems only yesterday that Hodges stood chatting in that easy, friendly, humble way of his. Even in kitchens you learn a lot about men. You learn who is going to stick to the job, who is going to do his part and a little bit more, and who is going to evade and throw clever little fastballs. Hodges scrupulously avoided 8:30 a.m. classes and all other tricks of getting away early after breakfast while his contemporaries worked on until 9:30 or 10 a.m. to finish the job. He was sure-handed; he was fast; he was eager; he was cheerful.

In fact, such work is most interesting if you feel you are doing it with a high degree of efficiency. When three young men wipe by hand within less than two hours all the dishes used by 500 people at a meal, they must exceed automobile assembly line speed and efficiency.

Hodges is the kind of man with the kind of easy stamina and friendliness you expect to last a long time. He doesn't seem subject to the kind of strains that shorten so many lives.

Luther Hodges was not unduly conspicuous for being a self-help student at Carolina. Over seventy percent of the 1,000 enrolled at Chapel Hill had some kind of part-time employment, either on the campus or in the downtown business block on Franklin Street. A senior at that time, Robert B. House, who later became chancellor of the university, wrote in a reminiscent mood: "About one fourth of us were adequately financed. Another one fourth were able to get along by strict economy and self-denial. The other half had to take advantage of every sort of job the community offered, and since such jobs were few they also had to borrow from the university loan funds or privately at home. Their education was never far above the bread and butter line."

Luther Hodges belonged to the "strict economy and self-denial" group described by Chancellor House. Of all students in that category, Luther stood out. "Even though I was a senior and paid little attention to freshmen, I was aware that Luther Hodges was around," said House. Young Hodges admired and tried to learn from older students. One among them was a sophomore, Albert Coates, who came from a farm in Johnston County, North Carolina. Coates was articulate, a good student, a debater, a political figure to be reckoned with on the campus and a witty and extravagant leader in formal discussions and bull sessions. He later studied law at Harvard, returned to Chapel Hill to teach law, and founded the Institute of Government at Chapel Hill.

As a sophomore, Coates' attention was attracted to freshman Luther Hodges. "Students from many walks of life came to Chapel Hill," said Coates. "The rich, the poor, the farm and town boys, but it was obvious that Luther Hodges was different and that he was respected. His force and vigor bowled you over. He was a stirrer-upper. Here was a boy who had come from work in a mill, with not much more than the clothes on his back, who was keeping up with the best of scholars. We applauded his merit."

The Swain Hall job was not enough to pay all Luther's expenses. He was offered a job firing the furnace at the Walter Dallam Toy residence on Franklin Street. Professor Toy taught German and was an administrator for the university, especially in getting jobs for worthy students. In getting Luther Hodges to carry out the ashes and to build the fires, Dr. Toy did himself as well as Hodges a favor. Luther hiked from Carr dormitory four blocks to the Toy home, arriving about 6 a.m. By the time the Toy family was up, the house was warm, and Luther was already at work in Swain Hall.

One job led to another, and Luther was called on to sit in faculty homes at nights while professors and deans and their wives attended concerts or engaged in other village social and professional and religious life. As an attendant for faculty children Luther was especially adept in walking and exercising Charlie Mangum, the young son of the Dean of the Medical School. Charlie, a spastic, later became a lawyer. Now over 60 years of age, Charlie Mangum refers to Luther Hodges—"He was a fine governor and Secretary of Commerce and industrialist, and he was a fine baby-sitter for me."

That first year in Chapel Hill was a struggle for Luther Hodges in balancing his studies, his extra-curricular interests, and his vital money-earning jobs. But Luther felt no pressure. As Leary Adams said, "He was sure-handed, he was fast, he was eager, he was cheerful—with the kind of easy stamina and friendliness you expect to last a long time." Luther Hodges knew he had found his niche in life at Chapel Hill. He was preparing for the success that had been prophesied by the Reverend Price Gwynn. The goal, though distant, was within his vision.

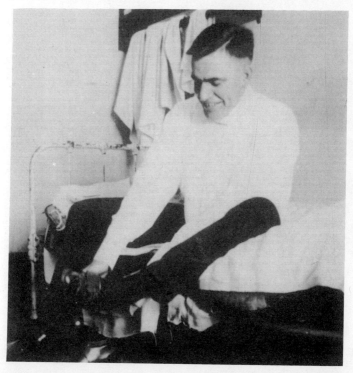

University of North Carolina student body president and senior class president Luther Hodges in his Vance Dormitory room in Chapel Hill, 1919.

Student Council at University of North Carolina in Chapel Hill in 1919. Luther H. Hodges, extreme right, first row, was President of the Senior Class and Student Body President. Top row, standing, left to right: W. M. York, Theodore Rondthaler, R. H. Griffith, Adam T. Thorp. Seated, left to right: J. V. Baggett, G. L. Nye, J. W. G. Powell and Luther Hodges. —Photo from 1919 Yackety Yack (student annual).

Chapter Four

"Best All-Around Student"

His name was William Stanley Bernard, and they called him "Bully." He taught Greek. Luther had done well in Latin and Greek in Leaksville, and he found himself living a fuller cultural life in the language classes at Chapel Hill. Bully Bernard was one of his favorite faculty members. Luther made A's in Professor Bernard's courses. He loved the discipline of the language, the demands on accuracy, and he relished the beauty and form of ancient prose and poetry. Professor Bernard honored good scholars and scolded bad students or lazy ones. "Bully," as the boys called him behind his back, was emotional and quick-tempered. Any ignorance made him irascible. In those days some professors wore detachable cuffs. When Dr. Bernard became angry in class he would lecture culprits blisteringly, call attention to errors, and demand better attention to studies—or else. At a crucial moment he would throw his arms up in a gesture that would cause his cuffs to suddenly protrude several inches out of his coat sleeves. This was known as "shooting the cuffs." After he had shot his cuffs, he would take the piece of chalk that he always carried in his hand, and he would turn and hurl the chalk at the blackboard. Then he would continue his protest about ignorance in his class. After putting on this act, for emphasis, he would cool off quickly. His linguistic point had been made. One student recollected, "I noticed that the bell never caught him in his wrath, and he never wounded except to correct, and he invariably said a healing word even as he gave a rebuke." He pronounced the word 'Greek' lovingly. His voice would click and trill on the 'G' and the 'r'. It would undulate and sing through the 'e's'. It would click again on the 'k'. Luther Hodges studied the dialogues of Socrates (in **Xenophon**) that first fall and studied Homer in the spring semester. In later years he became better acquainted outside class with Professor Bernard, and the friendship lasted. Bully Bernard was a memorable scholar. In 1916, another freshman came to Chapel Hill from Asheville, studied under Bully Bernard and remembered his old professor in a great American novel. Thomas Wolfe, a contemporary of Luther Hodges' in the University of North Carolina, gave Bully Bernard a fictitious name in his novel, **Look Homeward, Angel.** Wolfe wrote:

Buck Benson was a little man in the middle-forties, somewhat dandified, but old-fashioned in his dress. He wore wing collars, large plump cravats, and suede-topped shoes. His hair was thick, heavily grayed, beautifully kept. His face was courteously pugnacious, fierce, with large yellow bulging eyeballs, and several bulldog pleatings around the mouth. It was altogether a handsome ugliness.

His voice was low, lazy pleasant, with an indolent drawl, but without changing its pace or its inflection he could flay a victim with as cruel a tongue as ever wagged, and in the next breath wipe out hostility, restore affection, heal all wounds by the same agency. His charm was enormous. He was a good Grecian—an elegant scholar.

Luther made the freshman basketball squad and became a member of the varsity team when he was a sophomore. He weighed 175 pounds and was five feet, ten inches tall. He was a good team player, dribbled and passed the ball with adeptness, was accurate in ringing baskets from the middle of the court as well as from the foul line. The same tremendous drive that was obvious in his studies and his campus chores was apparent on the basketball team. He played basketball all four years at Carolina. In baseball he played well but did not have the same interest in it that he had in basketball. Luther had always wanted to be a pitcher, but he did better in the role of catcher. When Luther was offered the opportunity to be manager, rather than a player, of the baseball team, he accepted the position.

His enterprise aided him in finding new kinds of jobs—and the money he needed to pay for his tuition and rent, his fees, his clothing and books. Luther worked for a "pressing" club. "I took pants from the dormitories to the pressing club and back again," he said. "We charged ten cents for each pair of pants pressed." He acted as agent for a shoe repair shop, collecting shoes, getting them half-soled, bringing them back, collecting his money and banking his commission.

In the campus YMCA Luther Hodges helped to organize a unique club. The Young Men's Christian Association was not only a place for moral and religious instruction. It was also the center of campus civic and political influence and was a training ground for good citizenship. The secretary of the YMCA was a 1918 graduate, Thomas C. Boushall, who later become a banker in Richmond, Virginia. With Boushall's encouragement Luther Hodges formed a group that could today be alphabetized under the title of SYT—Save Your Time. About twenty students at the "Y", under Hodges' influence, met once a week to plan their schedule for the following seven days. They set down a schedule of their class and out-of-class working hours, and they budgeted the time they would spend in preparing lessons for the next day—so much time in the library, so much on each course of study. They outlined every fifteen minutes of the day. Having planned their work, they then worked their plan, and had plenty of time to spare for athletic games, literary societies, social activities and the gamut of Carolina life. It meant setting priorities on what had to be done. Luther Hodges found the Save Your Time club a valuable necessity to live the full life at the University, and he enlisted the cooperation and companionship of like-minded young men to work with him—for their mutual morale and efficiency.

Luther fell in with a crowd from Winston-Salem, North Carolina. One of his close friends was

Theodore Rondthaler. Rondthaler's grandfather was a bishop in the Moravian Church. Theodore's father (Howard) also became a bishop. Another companion was Curtis Vogler. Another in the group was Hilton West of Greensboro. Rondthaler became editor of the Carolina Magazine, the campus literary publication, and in later life he was a leader in North Carolina public schools.

In the Methodist and YMCA activities, Luther was regular in attendance and in teaching a Sunday School class. For a time he joined a group interested in foreign missions and once aspired to be a missionary. He was already a good student of the Bible and of church literature, and he came to know doctrines of other denominations and religions which he learned to respect. "I found that being a Methodist was not the only road to Heaven," he said.

In the summer between his first and second year at Carolina, Luther returned to Leaksville and worked in the mill at Spray. He saved enough money so that he felt more comfortable and freer from pressure when he came back to the campus as a sophomore. In his second summer he took a job as a salesman for a photographic concern, the Chicago Portrait Company. He describes his work:

> I got a commission on all completed and collected sales. We dealt in portraits and what is called black and white, also sepia, a colored picture which was very beautifully done. I would go into a house and persuade the mother or some member of the family to let me have a favorite photo of their father or mother or child or baby and would quote them from $2.95 up to

$5.95 depending on the color. But I was told never to mention the fact that they would be delivered in the frame. The frame showed it off best, but had not been included in the originally quoted price. I then had to make the second sale —the frame. It cost more than the picture. Always there was a protest, but usually they took the picture and the frame.

In this salesmanship Luther once ran into unexpected sales resistance that overpowered him. "Business got bad one part of the summer," he said, "and the company offered to reproduce the picture of a baby, or anyone else in the family, on a sofa pillow top. This could be done for one dollar. I sold this idea to a buxom, muscled woman who gave me the only picture she had of her baby. When I delivered the pillow top, keeping the baby's picture in my pocket, she said, "The picture ain't no good."

"It's all right," said Luther. "You'll have to take it, or you can't get your baby's picture back."

Then the storm struck. Hodges remembers it like this: "I hadn't reckoned with an irate mother before. Before I knew what happened I was lying on the floor from a flying wedge she had performed, and she had taken the picture out of my pocket and told me to get out of the house—which I did with alacrity."

In his third summer Luther sold Bibles and war history books. He started out each Monday morning in rural Virginia country with a knapsack over his shoulder and with war histories and Bibles in another container. "I never knew where the next meal was coming from," he said, "or where I would sleep at night. I knew I would not get back to my rooming house until Friday afternoon. It was poor country which I had picked out erroneously from a map. I hadn't gone into the economics of the county. They were poor farmers, owners and tenants. Many times I slept in the barn in the hayloft. But most of the time they took me in and let me sleep on a pallet in one of the rooms of the house."

Luther Hodges feels that his experience of summer selling taught him as much and gave him as much confidence for later selling, for getting along with people, as anything that happened in his subsequent life.

Back in Chapel Hill, Luther learned more of the lore of the campus. He understood the meaning of university traditions and the meaning of excellence in academic standards. What Edward Kidder Graham had said that first day about "standards of judgment" Luther came to comprehend in broader detail, together with a new realization about this pony-sized university that was growing rapidly into an institution of national stature. In the first part of the 20th Century, the University of North Carolina was actually not a full-blown university, but an excellent college of liberal arts and sciences, and the beginnings of professional schools and colleges. In four years after Luther Hodges was graduated, the University at Chapel Hill achieved its national status. It was accepted into membership in 1923 in the Association of American Universities, an exclusive group of high-ranking universities that even in 1968 has only 44 members in the entire nation. Many of the faculty who helped build the university to its eminence in the 1920's were already in Chapel Hill while Hodges was an undergraduate, and he had the benefit of their men-on-the-move dynamism and scholarship.

Luther was smitten by the everlasting beauty and isolation and academic integrity of the place. Along with debate teammate Thomas Wolfe, who was also editor of the student newspaper, **The Tar Heel,** Luther thought of the university as a place where he belonged. He felt he could, after a few years, come home again to Chapel Hill. In his **Look Homeward, Angel,** Tom Wolfe expressed it:

> The university was a charming and unforgettable place . . . in the little village of Pulpit Hill (Chapel Hill), in the central midland of the big state . . . the university was buried in a pastoral wilderness, on a long tabling butte, which rose steeply above the country. One burst suddenly, at the hilltop, on the end of a straggling village street, flanked by faculty houses, and winding a mile into the town center and the university. The central campus sloped back and up over a broad area of rich turf, groved with magificent ancient trees . . . There was still a good flavor of the wilderness about the place— one félt its remoteness, its isolated charm. It seemed like a provincial outpost of great Rome: the wilderness crept up to it like a beast.

In this pulsating university there were other faculty members: geologist Collier Cobb, mathematician Archibald Henderson, education specialist Marcus C. S. Noble, chemist Charles H. Herty, botanist W. C. Coker, librarian Louis Round Wilson, zoologist H.V.P. (Froggy) Wilson, psychologist Harry W. Chase. But there were two more that stirred Luther to thought and action, and these were Horace Williams, the philosopher, and Edwin Greenlaw, the English scholar. Williams was a homespun philosopher, an earthy man who employed the tenets of Hegel in day-to-day applications familiar to everyone. He was popular among most of the students, and they sought his advice, in and out of class. Generations of students were known as "Horace's Boys," and they credited Williams with furnishing them with a philosophy that guided their lives. But some of Professor Williams' illustrations rubbed certain of the young men the wrong way; they considered some of his questions and observations ridiculous. Horace didn't give such students good grades. Theodore Rondthaler's father, Howard Rondthaler, many years earlier was kept from making Phi Beta Kappa because he refused to reply to Williams' question: "Mr. Rondthaler, what does a horse think about when he sees a beautiful sunset?" Howard Rondthaler refused to consider the idea. Followers of Horace Williams declared his antics were only to prod students into thinking in unorthodox channels, to stretch their minds into greater flexibility. Others just considered him corny. Some were able to attend the class, observe and participate without becoming a disciple or a scornful critic. Luther Hodges was in the latter group. He enjoyed Horace without becoming involved.

Luther's favorite was Edwin Greenlaw, who taught Elizabethan literature. The main stress in the fall was on Spenser and in the spring on Bacon. Greenlaw synthesized the humanities and scientific culture from the Hebrews, the Greeks and Romans with the poets and playwrights of 18th century England. "Greenlaw was a loveable combination of sentimental boy and hard-boiled executive," observed Chancellor House. Both Greenlaw and Williams were searchers after truth, but they approached it from opposite directions. Horace Williams had his own system; he didn't recommend so much reading, and he loathed footnotes. Greenlaw produced documents and insisted that his students approach tasks by straight-line hard laborious methods, complete and accurate in every detail. There was no twisting and turning or endeavors to baffle the student in Greenlaw's makeup. He was out to enlighten, to clear away the darkness, to test and prove by clear examples steeped in the traditions of other disciplined scholars who had gone before. Greenlaw laid the foundations, in the English Department, for two substantial growths in the university—the Journalism School and Dramatic Arts. He set the plan for the Graduate School through which the University of North Carolina later emerged into national stature. He advocated the strenuous life of toil and research balanced with good teaching. There was no dichotomy of teaching on the one hand and research on the other, nor did he see a confrontation or a battle between a professor and a student to choose between teaching and research. A scholar does both. Greenlaw helped Luther Hodges to thrust forward into a philosophy of life and learning that shaped the young man's future.

In April 1918, Luther Hodges was in the throes of campus political elections. Theodore Rondthaler, Hilton West and half a dozen others became jubilant supporters of their candidate for president of the senior class of 1919. Luther Hodges was their man.

The campus swirled with war talk, and the Student Army Training Corps (SATC) was already a formidable part of university life. When the United States declared war on Germany, Luther and his classmates were celebrating local election victories and the prospect of coming victories in France. Elected to the presidency of his class also meant being president of the Student Government in the university.

However, Luther didn't return that fall. He enlisted for Army officer training in the summer and drilled and studied at Plattsburg, New York. From Plattsburg Training Camp, Second Lieutenant Hodges was sent to Camp Grant, Illinois. "My commanding officer was named Captain Robert E. Lee," said Hodges. He considered it remarkable that another officer at Camp Grant whose name was Captain Ulysses S. Grant was transferred by the Army to Camp Lee in Virginia. "My Captain Lee was a tobacco-smoking, cussing guy who was a helpful officer," said Hodges. "He taught me to do hand-to-hand bayonet fighting, as well as other elements of warfare."

The 1918 influenza epidemic hit the nation, including Camp Grant. "We lost 1,200 boys by death from flu in our camp that fall," said Hodges. Lieutenant Hodges was called upon to serve as a medic.

He tended the sick and was exposed to the deadly viruses. But Luther maintained his health. The toll among soldiers shocked him, but his greatest jolt came in news from Chapel Hill, North Carolina. President Edward Kidder Graham died in October of influenza.

Luther Hodges presided over the student body and the senior class when they assembled back in Chapel Hill in January, 1919. A memorial service for their great mentor and friend, Edward Graham, was the principal order of business. One day Luther Hodges and Theodore Rondthaler walked to the old Chapel Hill Cemetery. They put flowers on the grave of their president, and then they sat on the ground by the gravestone. They talked about the chapel talks and the lessons they had learned from Graham. They discussed immortality, and they explored the possibility that sometime they would meet again.

Although he had missed the fall term, Luther made up for the lost time by taking extra courses. He was slightly ahead of himself anyhow, having taken two extra courses during his junior year. This was his final year on the varsity basketball team. He was president of the Dialectic Senate, and agreed to be manager of the baseball team again.

Tar Heel Managing Editor, Tom Wolfe, published a letter January 17, 1919, signed by L. H. Hodges, President of the Student Body. The headline was "The University's Honor System." It read:

> To work with others in perfect harmony; to trust implicitly your fellow student; to have free expression; to live the fullest and finest life;

these are the expressions of our own Carolina
Honor System.

The Honor System is a thing to be lived and
not defined. When one attempts to give it a def-
inition he loses the richness of its spirit and
influence.

The highest expression of the Honor System
at Carolina is found in the full free life of a
Gentleman whose interests are bigger than the
man. A true Gentleman is an exponent of the
Honor System.

In the **Yackety Yack** of 1919, beside his picture,
the editors said of the Class President, Luther Hartwell Hodges:

Break into Carolina life anywhere and you
will discover 'Luke.' He has embued the entire
campus with his enthusiastic spirit. Luke will
make good. He is the best all-around man in our
class.

Then Luther received the ultimate accolade. He
was tapped into the Order of the Golden Fleece. In
the annual ceremonies in Memorial Hall where the
campus community had assembled, giant hooded
"Argonauts" marched in silence, symbolizing Greek
mythology's Jason and his search for the Golden
Fleece. Selection into the Fleece was considered the
highest honor to which a Carolina student could
aspire. At the tappings that night, Luther Hodges
name was at the top of the list.

Chapter Five

Luther Persuades and Learns

President Harry Woodburn Chase, a cigarette held lightly in his fingers, stood at the door of his office in South Building and spoke a few jovial words to President Luther Hodges. Chase had succeeded to the Presidency of the University following the deaths of President Graham and then Graham's successor, Marvin Hendrix Stacy. Chase was a New Englander, a suave scholar with zeal and the dedication to the idea that the University of North Carolina should not settle just to be a good university in North Carolina, nor a good southern university, but a university of the highest universal standards. Chase was to complete the building of the university in the next few years and go on to the University of Illinois and then to New York University. The two presidents, one of the university and the other of the student government and senior class, understood and respected each other. Luther Hodges' understanding of his fellow students helped President Chase in his own adjustment in his relations with faculty, students, alumni and the public.

When Luther reached Vance Dormitory, where he lived in his senior year, a letter awaited him. It was from Leaksville, from the Reverend Price Gwynn. Reverend Gwynn explained that the commencement speaker for the graduation exercises of Leaksville High School had cancelled. Would Luther come home and deliver the commencement address?

Luther did. He was introduced by Superintendent Gwynn, and made a good speech, demonstrating the new powers of rhetoric he had learned in the Dialectic Senate, in presiding at the YMCA and student council, in Greek under Bully Bernard and in the organized perspective under Edwin Greenlaw. It was a classical address by a smart young man. On the platform that day was a young history teacher, Martha Blakeney. She was twenty-two years old, and a 1918 graduate of the Woman's College in Greensboro. Her home was in Monroe, and Leaksville High was her first teaching job. She greeted young Hodges, also twenty-two, cordially and congratulated him for his well-organized speech and message.

At the mills in Leaksville and Spray, Luther called on his old friends. They welcomed him. Not only that, but he was urged to come back to Leaksville after his graduation. He had a future with the company, he was assured. Luther thanked them. He had not yet fully made up his mind, and when he was back in Chapel Hill again he considered his prospects.

"You can get this job in Alabama," he was told. The University of Alabama's YMCA needed a man of Hodges' enthusiasm and training. The job paid

$3,000 a year. "It was more money than I had ever heard of," said Hodges.

But there was also an opening at the Carolina Cotton and Woolen Company in Spray, one of many companies controlled by Marshall Field and Co. One of the managers, J. W. (Bill) East told Luther that the general manager had an opening on his staff, as administrative secretary. The job paid $83 a month, or $1,000 a year. That was one-third as much as he could make if he went into YMCA work in Alabama. Luther pondered his decision.

Finally the day came when Luther had to make his decision whether to take the $3,000 a year job in Alabama, or the $1,000 a year opportunity in Spray.

"This was one of the first major decisions I ever made," he said. "I had to analyze it—what choice I should make, and how it would come out. I finally decided that the $3,000 job would never amount to much more than $3,000 because of the nature of the work, but the job in the mills ought to amount to much more than $3,000 sometime if I did a good job."

But Luther had another reason. "Furthermore, I wanted to see if I could go back to the hometown, where I had scads of relatives, and to see if I could make good in the textile industry there."

Luther wrote his message of acceptance on a penny postcard, addressing it to L. W. Clark, the General Manager. The time set for his first day of work was August 5, 1919. (He had previously agreed to take another job for June and July.)

L. W. Clark was a Bostonian. He had had his training in New England mills and textile schools and knew the business thoroughly. In his New England accent he spoke of the several "plawnts" in Spray and Draper. Because of his accent and his bearing it was said of Mr. Clark, "He can strut sitting down."

"Your desk is in my office," said Clark. It was a brand new desk, in a corner opposite Mr. Clark's own desk, with a lovely roller top of oak. On Luther's desk was a typewriter with a wide carriage.

"You are my general assistant," said Clark. "You will just do everything for me that I need." This included writing reports about mill production and other activities which Clark made to the absentee owners of the mills in Chicago and New York.

That suited Luther. But he wanted to do more. "I can get all this done in the morning," he said. "I wonder if I could work in the mills in the afternoons. I'd like to know more than I do about what goes on inside the mills and I want to know the people."

Clark was skeptical at first. But Luther was persuasive. He convinced his boss that he would be more valuable to him if he spent at least a part of his time as a worker in the mill. "Although I had worked as a kid, I still needed to learn how to fix looms," he said. "I wanted to know what the problems of the people were, at first hand."

Clark finally agreed to let Luther work for six months on the half and half basis—mornings in the office, afternoons in the mill. One of Luther's tutors in the mill was Bud Burnett, an unlettered, pleasant, heavy-set, tobacco-chewing man. He taught Luther how to fix looms. Besides boning up on weaving and spinning and how to work with men and women in the mill, Luther "learned the ropes" from Bud Burnett in a dozen ways only known to men of experience.

Luther mastered the use of the typewriter. All reports, letters and facts about the mill's operations went through his hands. When meetings and conferences were held, Luther was on duty as secretary and reporter. This was before the days of tape recorders. Luther was disappointed when he found he couldn't get the information down fast enough— who said what, who replied and **exactly** what was spoken. His sense of recall was good, but he believed in the maxim of the ancient Chinese philosopher, "The palest ink is better than the most retentive memory." He wanted to get it down faster—all of it. The only answer was shorthand. He completed a shorthand course through the International Correspondence School in Pennsylvania. After that, Luther never missed a quotation, or a sentence, or a word. Nothing was left undone.

As he rose into greater prominence in the company, Luther Hodges was one of a new breed of mill managers living in a new day. The era of oppressed workers, child labor, long hours for women, and pittance pay was changing! His six months in the mill and his overall view of the mill's practices of the whole management exposed what seemed a fundamental fault in hiring and firing. Getting new

employees was haphazard; foremen often hired relatives and friends. Qualifications, experience, training
and aptitude often took second place to lesser cri-
teria. A well-qualified, bright young man might be
rejected because he didn't know anyone, and lacked
pull. Personnel policy, if any, was based not on **what**
but **whom** you knew. "There was little scientific
approach," said Hodges. "There was little efficiency.
There were no personnel records."

He decided to install a personnel system. It was
the first personnel department in the organization,
and one of the first in the South. He remembered
a young man he had known on the debating team
at Chapel Hill, William Bobbitt of the class of 1921.
Bobbitt was hired to come to Spray and help Hodges
set up records and a system of recruitment and employment based on merit. Bobbitt later went into
law, became a judge and now serves as a Justice in
the North Carolina Supreme Court.

The Hodges and Bobbitt system of personnel
curtailed the practice of nepotism in the mills. The
changeover was not easy. Luther Hodges himself had
scores of relatives in the tri-cities of Leaksville,
Spray and Draper. If he were to stop the hiring of
kin people among foremen and supervisors and
workers, he also had to be sure he set the example.
He refused to exercise any influence at all in favor
of family, friends, nephews and cousins. He said, "I
made the rule and stuck to it; never to extend a
favor or preference for a job or promotion to anyone
in any way related to me. I learned the lesson of no-
conflict-of-interests early because I was thrust into

it. It helped me all the rest of my life. I found no final resentment from the relatives and the proper respect, after the first shock, from associates. Some of them thought I ought to be a little more yielding for the sake of my relatives."

Luther could say "no" softly and smilingly—and firmly.

The young man entered into the life of the community. He went to church, taught a Sunday School class, assisted in boys' work at the YMCA. He played on the YMCA's young men's basketball team. He wrote to Chapel Hill and asked if his Leaksville cage squad could get a game against the White Phantoms, the varsity squad for the University of North Carolina. Yes, the Carolina team was willing to play the Hodges' "Y" team. The UNC basketball team was one of the finest in the entire southern region, but the "Y" team was making things rather hot for them early in the game. One flurry of action, and there was an accident. Billy Carmichael, star forward on the Carolina team, was playing opposite Luther Hodges. In a scramble under the basket, Carmichael's elbow came down and smacked Hodges in the mouth, knocking a front tooth out and on to the floor of the gymnasium. Luther retrieved the tooth and the game went on. A dentist replaced the tooth with a piece of silk thread, and it lasted for several years.

Almost forty years later when Hodges was Governor of the state of North Carolina he sat in the Governor's Box at a basketball game and watched the game. A sports reporter asked the Governor how he liked the action. Hodges replied that the players were too polite to one another and that the athletes were effete as compared with the old days. "It's a game of pansies," he told the reporter. "I don't like this blowing of whistles whenever anybody touches someone with their fingers or hands." The Governor told the reporter of his "Y" mill team playing against Carolina and how Billy Carmichael knocked his tooth out.

A couple of days later, after the sportswriter had published his dialogue with the governor, William D. Carmichael Jr., Vice President of the Consolidated University of North Carolina and the Billy Carmichael who had been the basketball star, telephoned Governor Hodges.

"Governor," said Carmichael. "Did you see Dante Germino's column about you in the **Durham Sun?**" The Governor had not. Carmichael related the colloquy.

"I have here a letter from a school teacher," said Carmichael. "She's upset because you won't recommend as much salary increases for teachers as she thinks you ought to."

The governor acknowledged that that could very well be so.

"Well, the teacher has sent me the sports column clipping, and she says this: 'Dear Mr. Carmichael: Why didn't you knock 'em all out?'"

Luther did not forget the pretty schoolteacher, Martha Blakeney, who had decorated the platform that day when he talked to the Leaksville High

School graduating class. She had become principal of the high school and at twenty-three was one of the most popular young women of the town. She had several suitors and escorts to events in the community and to social events in the state.

"This young lady looked awfully pretty to me," said Hodges. "But she wasn't enthusiastic about my wanting to date her, at first."

Their courtship included reading together, and sometimes Luther would help Martha with her school reports. Martha was not inclined at the outset to marry the young man. She told associates, "Under no condition will I marry that Luther Hodges." But she changed her mind. She succumbed not only to one of the super-salesmen of the 20th century, but to her own emotions and to the realization, shared by others, that here was a young man who would amount to something. Certainly he would be manager of the mills, and more. They were married June 24, 1922. Theodore Rondthaler was Luther's best man.

On their honeymoon trip, Martha and Luther visited Niagara Falls, New York City, and the town of East Aurora, New York. At East Aurora was the bookbinding and handicrafts showplace called Roycroft, founded by the author and advertising man, Elbert Hubbard. Martha and Luther had read Elbert Hubbard together, and a stay at Roycroft's pleased both of them.

To finance his honeymoon, Luther had sold a lot he had purchased the year before. On their way home the honeymooners took the night boat from

New York to Norfolk. It was on the boat that Luther realized that he was down to his last few dollars! He wondered whether he would have enough money to eat and pay for the train trip back home after they reached Norfolk.

It was at this moment that Martha became seasick. Food seemed unattractive to her. Luther went alone to the dining room. Frugally, he rejected the expensive items on the menu. He ordered only hash brown potatoes. When they reached Norfolk, Luther spent almost all his remaining cash for the two tickets to Danville and thence to Leaksville by the local Dick & Willy train. Luther didn't let Martha know how close his pocketbook was to absolute zero. They walked to the diner on the train. Luther insisted that Martha have the best. She noticed that he ordered hash brown potatoes. "I **like** hash brown potatoes," he explained to her.

They arrived at the Colonade Hotel in Spray where they spent the first few weeks of married life, and after tips were paid Luther found that he had five cents left in his pocket. The next day at the mill his monthly check was awaiting him. But it had been a close call.

Chapter Six

"Let Luther Do It"

When John Hodges gave up farming in Virginia and moved across the boundary line into North Carolina to the mill villages of Spray, Draper and Leaksville, he was following the country-to-town wave of migration which has been a part of the South's history since the 1870's.

Farms became mechanized. It required fewer people to do the necessary work to raise food and other agricultural products. Unemployment resulted. Men who tilled the soil got low prices for their products. Hard times were especially tragic in the South where there was little industry to balance the agricultural economy. The few textile mills established in the South prospered. The destitute men and women on the farms were eager for any kind of work, and they were willing to labor for low wages. They moved from the farms to the mill towns. Entreprenuers found that labor costs in the South and the new and modern machinery of the southern mills gave them a distinct advantage over mills of

New England where labor costs were high and machinery old. Compared with mills in Massachusetts, New Hampshire, Rhode Island and other northern states, southern mills could sell textile products cheaper. The long-term result has been a comparative decline in the New England textile industry and emergence of the South as the nation's greatest textile region. Although political leaders of the North have pointed the finger of scorn at the South for low-wage policies and therefore lower standards of living compared with other parts of the United States, it is realistic to recognize that the people of the South would be in even worse condition and there would be even more marked differences in per capita wealth between the South and the nation as a whole, if it had not been for the growth of the textile industry in the South. The specter of farm unemployment continues still, and population experts predict that migration from farm to cities and from the South to other parts of the nation will continue for the next quarter of a century at least, probably up to the year 2000.

Luther Hodges' father and brothers and sisters who worked in the mills of Spray, North Carolina, were doing what tens of thousands of victims of the Industrial Revolution had been forced to do. They moved from farm to town and bettered their condition, but not much.

Child labor and long hours for women were practices that were already on the way out by the time Luther Hodges came back home from the university in 1919.

"Let's let Luther do that," said L. W. Clark one day. It was not the most pleasant task in the mill, and four or five other men might have drawn the chore. But he knew that Luther would do it without complaining and would do it well. Clark's instructions became a byword—"Let Luther do it."

Luther did it. He turned service into leadership. He found that leaders were not to stand in front and order others. They were more; leaders were men who could also serve others. Luther Hodges was that kind of leader.

"Luther asked questions," said Martha Hodges. "When he met someone who knew some special skill or who had mastered a technique, he kept asking that man questions to find out just how it was done." His interest in other people was concentrated on finding out what they knew. He respected a man of ability, whether it was an expert lawyer, doctor, plumber, mechanic or loom fixer. Self-improvement was behind his probing.

Luther and Martha lived in a small house that the mill had built for them. It was big enough to be comfortable in when their two daughters were born, Betsy in 1925 and Nancy in 1926. Luther was a prodigious worker in the mill, and he remained involved in extracurricular activities: the American Legion, YMCA, Boy Scouts, local politics, church work. His life was crammed full, just as it had been at Chapel Hill.

But in 1923, Luther found an extra special outside interest that transcended all of the others. Rotary clubs were being founded all over the nation, and Luther was attracted to the idea of a civic club. Of all the community service organizations he saw, his preference was for Rotary. With a group of other men he organized a club in Leaksville, and was its first secretary and treasurer. Luther became president of the Leaksville Club in 1927 and then became District Governor for most of the state of North Carolina. He delighted in the fellowship, the practice of calling other members by their first names, the conviviality and the principles that were central to the idea of Rotary.

When he became busier and busier with the management of the mills and was called upon daily for a myriad of religious and civic and fraternal tasks, he decided that he would have to budget his time—as he had done at the university. So, Luther again set priorities. After his work, his number one priority, he concluded, would be Rotary. "I obtained more satisfaction from serving in Rotary than I had in any other of my interests," he said. "I made up my mind that although I would minor in many service activities, I would major in Rotary."

When Luther began to work in L. W. Clark's office, that mill and several others of Leaksville and Spray and Draper were controlled by Marshall Field and Company of Chicago. Some of the mills had been founded in the 1890's and had merged and separated and joined again. Some had gone bankrupt and had to be rescued financially. Marshall Field and Company had advanced money and merchandise. When the advances on American Warehouse Company of Spray reached $900,000 in May 1910,

Marshall Field purchased the controlling stock and took over the company.

In a history of the North Carolina and Virginia mills of Marshall Field and Company written by E. D. Pitcher, salient facts about the seventeen original mills were described.

Mr. Pitcher wrote:

A problem that Marshall Field & Company had was to improve the quality of the product. The former owners were content to turn out anything that would sell at some price and that was one of the reasons why they did not succeed.

Early owners of the American Warehouse Company which became a finishing plant included Benjamin N. Duke, James B. Duke, J. Pierpont Morgan and John M. Studebaker. Some of the other mills were at first locally owned, including the Nantucket Mills, headed by B. Frank Mebane, the man who had given Luther Hodges and his classmates the quarters in exchange for political influence over their fathers. Mr. Mebane also was president of the Lily Mill, the Spray Woolen Mills, the German-American Company and the Rhode Island Mill.

The 17 mills of Leaksville, Spray and Draper— and later mills at Fieldale and Roanoke, Virginia, and High Point, North Carolina—(all of which eventually became a part of the Marshall Field Corporation) manufactured such things as rugs, blankets, sheets, towels, gingham, dresses, outing flannels, bedspreads, sleeping garments, upholstery, hosiery, underwear and other clothing and furnishings.

Marshall Field had earlier taken over fiscal control of the Carolina Cotton and Woolen Mills Co., of Spray. Historian Pitcher writes:

> For several years Marshall Field and Company had been buying blankets, gingham and flannels from the Mebane group of mills at Spray and Draper, advancing money directly to the mills for purchase of raw material and payment of labor, and also making direct loans. By reason of unacceptable merchandise in 1908 the advances had increased to such an extent it was thought advisable to have a representative in close touch with the operations . . .

Luther Hodges advanced from secretary to the general manager of the Marshall Field mills. He became manager of the blanket mill in 1927. He was promoted in 1934 to production manager of all mills in the Leaksville area. In 1938 he was elevated to the position of manager of all 29 Marshall Field mills in the United States and abroad. In 1940 he moved his headquarters from Leaksville to New York City. He became Vice President of Marshall Field & Co. in 1943. He retired from the company in 1950.

These **Who's Who** abbreviated vital statistics relate the milestones in Luther Hodges thirty-one years with one of the nation's largest manufacturing enterprises. Beneath the list of promotions in his rise up the ladder to success is the story of Luther Hodges, the man.

Harold Whitcomb was manager of an enterprising small family-owned textile plant in Franklin,

New Hampshire. He read in the **Daily News Record,** the national textile journal, that managerial jobs "for ambitious young fellows" might open up in the Marshall Field and Company, since Luther Hodges had become general manager. That was in 1938. Through mutual acquaintances, Whitcomb and Hodges established contact, and they arranged to meet at the Statler Hotel in Boston. They talked for three hours, about textile manufacturing and people and economics. They discussed Rotary. Whitcomb was president of the Rotary club in Franklin, N. H. "It didn't hurt me," he said. "Hodges was all business. He wasn't encouraging," said Whitcomb. "He told me there might be something to come up, that Marshall Field was going to make a few changes, and would need some people."

When they parted, Hodges said to Whitcomb, "You'll hear something, one way or the other, pretty soon."

Several days later Hodges phoned. It was seven o'clock in the morning. He offered Whitcomb the assistant managership of the Lumb Knitting Company in Pawtucket, Rhode Island. Ralph Lumb, the manager, would step out as head of the mill in a few weeks and Whitcomb would succeed him.

Whitcomb told Hodges he would like to think it over, that the owners of the mill in Franklin had been good to him, both in business and personally.

"How long would you want to take to think it over?" asked Hodges.

"About a week?" suggested Whitcomb.

"We can't wait that long!" said Hodges. "How about letting me know something Monday morning? I believe you want to come with us. My experience has been that if you want to do a thing, do it."

Whitcomb made his decision. He gave a month's notice to the Franklin Mill and moved to Pawtucket. A year later Hodges brought Whitcomb to Leaksville and made him director of purchases of raw materials and supplies. Whitcomb was experienced in all aspects of textiles, but his major efforts were in manufacturing and production. He worked with Luther Hodges during the next fifteen years.

"Luther Hodges is one of the best executives I have ever known," said Whitcomb. "He is well-organized. He wastes no time. During office hours there was no small talk. He was strictly business." Luther Hodges made things move.

Each of Hodges' staff had a regular appointment once a week to talk over company business as it affected them. In between the weekly conferences were intermittent meetings, phone contacts and emergency appointments. But the weekly conferences were a regular part of the management routine. He kept a file on each of the men responsible to him. Letters and reports went into the individual files, and Hodges had all the information on his desk when time for the interviews came.

"You could take up anything with him at these conferences," said Whitcomb, "The matters on the agenda and new business."

Harold Whitcomb found that Luther Hodges grasped facts quickly. He sifted through many ideas rapidly—considering, rejecting, accepting. "He didn't take long to make up his mind," said Whitcomb. "He didn't rush into decisions. He heard all sides, asked questions, and thought it over. Then he decided."

Hodges was not one to retreat when he ran into obstacles. Opposition didn't deter him. "If he could not do a thing one way," said Whitcomb, "He'd try another. He never gave up."

In his daily management of the plants, the production, the sales, the advertising and other facets of the business, Luther Hodges seldom relaxed. "He was taut as a G-string," said Whitcomb. His high-strung temperment was apparent in little ways too. "He carried watches," said Whitcomb, "and he swung the chain. Or he'd swing the keys on the chain. Or a stone attached to the watch chain. He never acted relaxed."

Hodges was straightforward in his relations in business. There was no subterfuge. "You always knew what he meant," said Whitcomb. "He made certain he was understood. He was no fence straddler. You knew when he was pleased or displeased."

Luther Hodges and his associates built up production and increased sales. Whitcomb transferred to New York with Hodges. The mills were working full blast. Hodges was also traveling extensively— selling, selling, selling. He negotiated large contracts with Sears and Roebuck, Penney's and other large chain establishments. The giant Marshall Field retail stores and outlets took only about five percent of the total production of the mills. The rest went into world markets. As Vice President of Marshall Field and Company and general manager of its worldwide manufacturing enterprises, Luther Hodges was one of the nation's foremost business executives, a man of skill and enlightened social consciousness, a cosmopolitan, a strict and self-disciplined manager who knew how to marshall the appropriate men and raw materials to get the maximum benefits in a free enterprise system.

Luther H. Hodges in 1945. He was 47 years old and Vice President and General Manager of Marshall Field and Co. in New York City and a director of OPA in wartime Washington, D. C.

Chapter Seven

Be Honest! Be Punctual! Be Busy!

Martha Hodges kept the home fire burning. While her busy husband worked and managed the mills all day and spent several evenings a week at Rotary, the American Legion, the YMCA, the Boy Scouts, local school activities, occasional hunting and fishing trips, church meetings and other civic interests, Martha joined in some of his town and community work and encouraged him in others. She worked with the Girl Scouts. She took art classes and painted dozens of canvases. Social life in the three small towns was active, and she joined study clubs, bridge clubs, church organizations. She accepted a part-time job tutoring boys and girls and advised them on vocations.

She considered her main task to be the wife of Luther Hodges, and she was confident that he was a man who would attain both material success and the achievement that derives from moral discipline and balanced civic and spiritual values. "He was idealistic," said Martha.

"One of my contributions was to pay the bills,"
she said. She managed the home. Martha was never
a nagging nor a demanding wife. When Luther was
racing ahead on a crowded schedule, she never at-
tempted to stop or curb any activities in her behalf. "I thought these things he wanted to do were
important, too," she said, "and I went along with
them."

When their two daughters were born, Betsy in
June of 1925, and Nancy in September 1926, Luther
took his fatherhood obligations with the utmost
seriousness. He played with them, and devoted a lot
of attention to them. "He never spanked one of them
in his life," said Martha. "If any spanking had to
be done, I did it. In later years when they were
growing up, he expected them to be obedient and
he would talk to them about good conduct and what
was expected of them. He always did this quietly and
firmly."

Outside the foursome of Luther and Martha's
little family, there was the larger Hodges family.
John Hodges, Luther's father, was now a member
of the Leaksville School Board. The strict days of
Luther's boyhood were no more, and the family got
together at outings, especially at Christmas time.
Luther visited his brothers and sisters. But even in
his familial assocations, Luther Hodges was orderly
as a stop-watch. "If Luther phoned to say he would
drop by at 11:30 and would stay half an hour," said
his sister, Ethel Edwards, "you knew he would be
ringing the doorbell exactly at 11:30 and that he
would be on his way again promptly at noon." Once

at a family reunion. John Hodges counted up the number of grandchildren. He named the progeny of Dave Hodges. Ethel Edwards, Beulah Haizlip, Blanche Crews, Annie Hopper, Ola Frazier, Lessie Marlowe, Luther and Munsey Hodges. The total was 49. "I think there should be fifty before I die." he said early in 1936. But John Hodges died early that same year, just before the birth of the fiftieth. Luther Hartwell Hodges Jr.

Sometimes the Luther Hodges family traveled together. Especially when Betsy and Nancy were older. They took the overnight train from Greensboro to New York, and Martha and the girls would find things to do while Luther attended to his business in the New York offices of Marshall Field and Co.

One day in New York City, Luther Hodges gave his daughters a practical lesson in independence, learning how to do things on their own. "I was twelve years old," said Betsy, "and Nancy was eleven. He gave us money to go to the Radio City Music Hall and a few dollars over. He told us he wanted us to come back to the hotel after the show. We didn't know how to find our way from the Music Hall to the Barclay Hotel on Lexington Avenue. He told us to figure out the best way and to make our own decision about how we'd get there. First, we thought of taking a cross-town bus, and then we considered how far it was and whether we could walk it. Finally, we took a taxi. He was very proud of us for thinking of it. It was a simple lesson in encouraging us to make a decision by choosing between several alternatives, but it is one that I remember well."

Luther Hodges played games with his children. He challenged them occasionally to a fast go at Ping-Pong. "He put pressure on us," said Betsy. "He played a good game and he'd try to win and usually did."

In such moments of family sport, Luther Hodges became relaxed. "He was a great kidder," said Betsy. "He would try to rattle me in the Ping-Pong game, would tell me I was going to miss. He'd drop his own paddle and pick it up again to distract my attention."

These pressures didn't bother her, but actually gave her strength, she said. She knew that this was exactly the intention of her father, to make sure she kept her poise. Competition was a sport and all members of the family practiced it. They competed, too, in grades in school and later in college. Luther Hodges insisted on excellence. He expected his children to make the honor roll. When they came home with a report card of A's and B's, there was no special praise. That was what they were supposed to make. But if there were C's or D's, they were in for a lecture on dedication to books and devotion to scholarship. Passing was not good enough. One hundred percent perfection was the goal, and Luther let them know it.

"Above all," said Luther to his daughters and to his son, "be honest in everything you do. Regulate your time and the things you must do. Don't go over-board on your special interests; don't be an extremist. Be prompt. Always be on time. Be fair in your dealings with others. Tell the truth. Work hard. Budget your time and your money."

Luther set up a savings account for each of his children, and they were counted on to earn and save and spend intelligently. When they went away to college, he established a special account for each of them—to carry them four years. "This is for your college expenses," he said. "You'll have to make a budget and make it last. It's yours to use as you see fit. There will be no more."

When the three Hodges children were graduated, each had money left in his college fund. "I am independent," said Betsy (now Mrs. Donald Bernard of Short Hills, New Jersey), "and I believe all of us have that sense of self-reliance." Betsy attended Salem Academy in Winston-Salem, Duke University and Sarah Lawrence College as a day student when the Hodges lived in New York. Nancy went to school at Vassar.

"Daddy always was (and, of course, still is) my friend as well as my father," said Nancy. "He tried to find time for a 'play' session with us. We learned from him many games of skill, but perhaps more important we learned sportsmanship. If one of us were a bad loser, we knew about it!"

It was Luther's custom to take both daughters to football games in Chapel Hill, beginning when they were under ten years old. "Somehow he could always find a parking space near the entrance gate," said Nancy. People would say he was lucky, to which he would reply: "You usually make your own luck.

Lucky things happen to people who make an extra effort."

One fall day in Chapel Hill, the Hodges family got caught in a traffic jam. Betsy was ten; Nancy was nine. Luther Hodges didn't sit in his car and wait for the football traffic to unsnarl. "He got out of the car and directed traffic until the jam was sorted out," said Nancy.

Although it was Martha Hodges' role to spank the children when it was needed, Nancy remembers that her father made an exception to the rule one day. She brought home some numbers from school, and proudly showed her facility in writing numbers, from one up to ten. Nancy had written all the numbers except the number 5; that had been written by the teacher. "I claimed the '5' was my own writing, too," said Nancy. "Daddy gave me a spanking. I don't remember ever telling a lie thereafter."

One of Luther Hodges' injunctions to his children was: don't use swear words. Nancy remembers "one day when I was sixteen my father was following me downstairs in our home. I tripped and landed on a previously injured knee, and knowing that meant I would miss a big 'prom' I weepingly cried 'damn!' Daddy walked right around me and out of the room, quietly remarking, 'I would help a **lady** to get up.' This I think, cured me of using swear words forever. He has certainly been the major influence in my life."

Of all his community activities Luther's main zest was in Rotary. When he became District Governor of Rotary in 1927, he visited clubs from one end of the state to the other and came to know the leadership in the state's towns and cities. He liked the service ideal as well as the conviviality and informality of Rotary meetings. A good speaker, his comments on civic and religious and universal affairs of mankind were enunciated in well-organized words and phrases and spoken in a smooth but quick-tempo delivery. His speeches had a straightforward impact, and his listeners respected and enjoyed him.

He joined the Democratic party and was active on the local level and later was called on for state-wide duties, particularly in vocational education and as a member of the State Highway Commission. He was elected to the Board of Trustees of the University of North Carolina. His progressive advocacy of improved schools advanced to the point that he was even impatient to make changes swiftly and sometimes without regard to personalities involved **—if it was for the public good.** Once Luther even found to his chagrin that in a public school controversy in Leaksville he was at odds with his old mentor, the Reverend Price Gwynn, now a banker. Notwithstanding, Luther spoke his mind at a public meeting, and after he had spoken, Mr. Gwynn arose to congratulate him.

In a tribute to Mr. Gwynn years after, Luther Hodges said in an address:

> I was privileged to sit at his feet and as I learned Greek I learned the value of character from him. Further, I learned an invaluable thing —the value of thinking and fighting for what you considered right, for that in which you be-

lieve, and I am happy to testify that he had been a tremendous influence in my life.

I had the honor and pleasure as a young devotee of his to fight on his side against arbitrary rules and strangling regulations.

Later on, I scrapped him, just as hard as I had helped him, when we found ourselves on opposite sides of the school improvement program. We fought openly and somewhat violently . . . I recall one particular instance, when I was making what I thought was a very strong argument against Mr. Gwynn, and it looked for a moment as if the tide would be turned. As I finished he arose quickly, and said: "That is a fine speech— he is one of my boys, and that is just the way I taught him to speak."

Martha Hodges was an excellent hostess and was called on to entertain visiting executives of Marshall Field and the company's customers. Leaksville had no hotel of the excellence comparable with places these men and their wives were accustomed to in larger cities, so the Hodges home had many overnight guests. In the New York years, they entertained at home and in the city. They maintained a cottage at Crescent Beach, South Carolina, and later they built a summer home at Linville in the North Carolina mountains. Luther was at first both hunter and fisherman, but finally he concentrated entirely on fishing at his vacation retreats. An admittedly impatient man, he found he could relax entirely while fishing. The drive and the pressure of business life were forgotten when he held a fishing line in his hands, or when he cast for fish in the ocean and mountain streams. The soothing balm of the fisherman's life continued afterwards when in the company of friends Luther cleaned and cooked the fish and served it with a special brand of hush puppies. In Hush Puppies **a la Hodges,** the corn meal is soaked in beer and onions.

Luther Hodges is an early riser, getting up about 6:30 in the morning and going to bed about 9 or 10 o'clock at night. Even if guests are present he will excuse himself. "It's my bedtime," he will announce at 10 p.m. Others present may continue the talk or the party, but Luther Hodges gets his sleep. He exercises, doing calisthenics daily, and his weight has never increased twelve pounds above that when he played basketball at Chapel Hill.

Once in their early days in Leaksville, Luther and Martha were invited by President Harry W. Chase to come to Chapel Hill where Luther was to speak on "The Carolina Spirit" at chapel. While they were there they visited the philosophy class taught by Professor Horace Williams. Martha Hodges remembers that she was not altogether impresed by Professor Williams' conduct that day. "He was arguing with Jonathan Daniels on what a horse thinks about cabbage," she said. "It seemed a little absurd to me."

As they walked around the campus at Chapel Hill, past the Old Well and across the greensward to the Davie Poplar, Luther said to Martha, "We'll come back to this place some day. We will live here in Chapel Hill." Martha knew that it was not just an idle observation, nor a spur-of-the-moment decision. She had already come to know that Luther Hodges meant exactly what he said. She knew, just as he promised, that they would be coming back to Chapel Hill to live some day.

Luther made the big decisions in the Hodges family. "He'd often consult me about things, but usually he made up his mind and said what we would do. Normally I liked to talk about the things leading up to a decision, but not Luther. But it didn't really matter. The things that Luther wanted to do were usually the things I wanted to do. He sometimes told me about big decisions in the business, because he knew I could keep a secret. He kept me informed, but his were the decisions—whether it was a change of jobs, or a vacation place, or other matters."

In minor matters and in running the home, Luther Hodges lets Martha have her own way. For example, Luther likes persimmons and persimmon pudding. Martha doesn't. "He decided he'd like to have persimmon pudding from the persimmon tree in the yard," said Martha. "I told him it was too messy fooling with persimmons," she said. "So, he gathered the persimmons, collandered the seeds out, brushed up on recipes and with the help of the cook made a persimmon pudding."

In the years when his children were growing up and Luther Hodges was growing ever stronger in the competitive world of American big business, life was often crowded. But Luther Hodges, in home life as in business life, was well organized. His children grew to be mature, handsome and successful—the two daughters in married life and his son as a civic-minded banker and articulate young leader in North Carolina's late 20th century life.

Luther Hodges Jr. was ten—eleven years younger than his two sisters. When he was himself in his teens and his sisters in the twenties and already married and with growing families, the Hodges family was scattered—Nancy in New Delhi, India, where her husband was with an oil company; Betsy in Short Hills, New Jersey; his father going into retirement with Marshall Field and Co., taking up a new career in the nation's service, in Marshall Plan work in Germany. As young Luther Hodges studied at Eaglebrook Preparatory School in Deerfield, Massachusetts, his father was going into politics in North Carolina, running for Lieutenant Governor. When Luther Jr. attended the University of North Carolina, his father was Governor of the state. At the time young Luther was graduated from the Harvard School of Business Administration, his father was Secretary of Commerce. A Leaksville home, a New York residence, the Governor's Mansion in Raleigh, and a Washington, D.C. address were heady abodes for a youth who had not as rigorous an upbringing as had his father. These were serious concerns, of father and son and mother. Could such a family produce useful citizens of balanced integrity? The answer is: It could, and did.

Faculty members at the University of North Carolina who had a profound influence on the college education of Luther H. Hodges. Top: William S. (Bully) Bernard, professor of Greek. Bottom: Edward Kidder Graham, president of the university.

Chapter Eight

Businessman in World War II

Newspapers customarily publish (at least once a year) a list of "high salaries" earned by prominent Americans. Information gleaned from public records available through tax agencies are featured on business pages. It was public knowledge that Luther H. Hodges' annual salary in the 1940's was in excess of $100,000 a year.

The family, living in Bronxville, New York, did not go overboard in extravagance. Modest and comfortable are the words for their mode of life. Betsy was at Sarah Lawrence College in the early days of World War II, and Nancy attended Vassar. When Luther obtained leave from Marshall Field and Company to do volunteer work for the government in 1944, Luther Jr. was only eight years old.

Just as he had been ready in 1918 in World War I, Luther Hodges was prepared and eager for service in World War II. "I'd like the toughest assignment you have available," Luther Hodges told men in government who sought talent. He was named Chief

of the OPA's price control for the entire textile industry. The Office of Price Administration existed to
keep charges to consumers from mounting beyond
reason in the wartime economic upheaval. He ad-
ministered controls on an annual business volume
of four billion dollars. "It probably wasn't the toughest assignment in Washington, but it was tough
enough," said Hodges.

Priding himself on swift movement and quick
decisions which therefore almost automatically made
red tape a natural enemy, Hodges often found himself battling on two fronts—against the normal
complications of price administration, difficult at
best, and against the snarls of routine and cumber-
some rules that slowed down the operations.

Even though he bucked against red tape and
promoted business-type efficiency in government,
Luther fell into a snare on one occasion. The experience made him wary of those who want to operate in
too much of a hurry when haste makes not only
waste but can lose the taxpayers' money. He tells
about it in a book he wrote, **The Business Conscience:**

> A group of acquaintances from the textile
> industry came into my office with a horror story
> about the bad treatment they were receiving
> from the agency. They pointed out that their
> urgent request for price relief was being shut-
> tled from post to pillar with no one taking the
> time to give them a fair hearing. They were be-
> ing put off, to the detriment of their stockhold-
> ers and their workers.
>
> I listened sympathetically to this account of
> frustrating inaction, then asked for facts about

their price situation. They supplied some information which seemed to back up their claim for relief. After that I was definitely leaning in their direction.

But then Luther Hodges decided to put the men on their honor before making a commitment. He looked from face to face and from eye to eye and asked, "Are you giving me the whole story? Are you telling me the whole truth? Can I count on the figures you've given me? Can I be assured that the relief you ask is fair to the government as well as to yourselves?"

Hodges was assured without equivocation that their facts were completely truthful and that he need have no fear on that account.

"All right," he said, "I'll put this thing through for you within forty-eight hours. I'll get you the answer and give you relief, because I want to see this thing move and I want to do the right thing." He added, "You realize I'm here as a public servant with some knowledge of the textile industry, but I do not know your particular case in any detail. I must take your word for what you've said." They assured him again he had nothing to worry about.

In writing later about business ethics, Luther Hodges tells the rest of the story:

> Despite strong protests from my associates and superiors in OPA, I pushed the case through to a final, favorable decision. I was quite proud of my success at snipping through red tape. It did not cross my mind that, as a newly-installed public servant, I should have dealt with my old friends at arm's length. I should have made

doubly certain that the information they presented was accurate.

Many years later, at a cocktail party, the leader of the delegation which had won my support took too many drinks and turning to his group of prominent associates said with great glee, "We certainly bilked old Luther out of more than a million dollars that day, didn't we, fellows?"

My friends had lied to me. They had taken advantage of my friendship and my sympathy.

It was a lesson Luther Hodges never forgot. It became a part of his ethical code to beware of a conflict of interests. He became as watchful as he had been careful to avoid nepotism in the early days as a mill manager in Spray. "Beware of friends—or ostensible friends"—became a watchword.

An OPA Administrator expressed his appreciation to Hodges for his excellent work in price administration. The day after he was out of the OPA job, a phone call came from Secretary of Agriculture Clinton Anderson. He wanted Hodges to be assistant secretary. Hodges declined. But he did agree to work with Anderson as a consultant and to investigate the money-lending Commodity Credit Corporation. Hodges' job was to find the inventory and verify the accounts. In six months this was complete. "Well done," said Anderson. Luther Hodges then returned to Marshall Field and Company which was just then making automation plans for post-war expansion.

In his travels for Marshall Field and Company, Luther found it useful to send back "Trip Reports" to other executives of the corporation. It was something about his calls on customers, his impressions of their market places and what it meant to the company's well-being. The Trip Reports elicited a good response and in 1947 Luther expanded the reports to include his wife and children, his brothers and sisters, other relatives and a few friends. For over twenty years, up to the present date, he wrote his impressions of people, places visited and interesting experiences as well as observations and philosophy from time to time as he traveled and saw the world.

A business trip combined with pleasure was the summer journey in 1947 to California, Oregon and Washington and on into Alaska. Martha and Luther took Nancy, who had recently been graduated from Vassar. Traveling by train, Luther recorded being met by Rotarians at Louisville, Kentucky, who wanted to show him the town. It was only 9:30 p.m. Louisville time. But they had not known of Luther Hodges' early-to-sleep policy. "If you don't mind, I'm going to bed," he said. "It's 11:30 by my time even though you show 9:30 by Louisville time." He described the new Sears escalator, the "first in Kentucky," and at Columbus, Ohio, he wrote of "The Wonder Store" operated by the Lazarus family. In San Francisco he called on Karastan customers (Karastan is a highly exotic and useful rug developed at Marshall Field's Leaksville plant in 1927), and he also celebrated with Martha their 25th wedding anniversary.

He golfed at Pebble Beach at Del Monte, California. "I won money but lost golf balls in the ocean," he noted in his Trip Report.

The Hodges family spent time at a mountain cabin in Alaska and nearby ran a stream brimming with trout and red snapper. Martha, he recorded, caught the biggest fish, a 16-pound snapper. In Jasper National Park's Bell Island they fished again. Here is an incident reported by Luther:

> I suggested to Martha that she sit on the bridge and hang her feet over the side. I immediately turned to assembling the trout rod and lines. A minute later I heard a scream and looked to see Martha in 20 feet of cold water. She had naturally assumed that a large log which had floated against the raft was a part of the bridge and had stepped on it. We pulled her out.

In later years, in party conversation, Luther amended his account of the incident. "When I first heard her call, I told her to wait just a minute until I could get my rod fixed, but she didn't think that was funny."

Although it was fun to catch the fish, Luther Hodges enjoyed the outing— even the occasional hardships—as much as reeling the fish in. He wrote: "Wednesday I had a lot of fun fishing near our cabin for brook trout and getting my line and fly in all the bushes and falling over the rocks and rapids."

In concluding the Alaskan trip report, Luther Hodges did a bit of editorializing on one of the things it means to be an American:

> It has been a grand trip but we shall be happy to get back. We are better Americans as

we have learned of more to appreciate especially as we see what others have and **don't have.**

Later in 1947, Luther flew to South America— to make advance plans as convention chairman for the International Rotary Convention of 1948 to be held in Rio de Janiero. In one stop where he heard of legends of the Indians of the Amazon River, he wrote:

> I was told one tribe who made "afternoon" hats of selected palm leaves and of the pleasure and effective designs they created. I asked him to send me one so that Marshall Field and Company, Retail, could take a look.

Luther Hodges never missed a business opportunity!

Stopping in Trinidad on the way home, he wrote:

> A sidewalk peddler offered me a silver bracelet "hand-made"—as I went into a store. When I came out he had reduced the price and when I still said 'no' and the car started he named (and got) a figure, exactly one-fifth of the orginal price.

In Rotary, Luther Hodges had served as a director of the New York City Club for three years and became President of the New York Club in 1946. Prior to that, Rotary called on him three times for international tasks since his term as District Governor in North Carolina: Chairman of the Rotary International Committee on Community Service, Rotary representative at the organization of the United Nations in 1945, and Chairman of the Post-War Committee of Rotary from 1943 to 1945. The presidency in 1946 of one of the world's greatest clubs, New York City Rotary, was one of the most satisfying opportunities for service he had experienced. This was followed immediately by being chosen chairman of the Rotary International Convention at Rio in May of 1948. He became a Director of Rotary International in 1953. Martha Hodges said years later, "I knew even then that Luther would someday be President of Rotary International. I wasn't surprised in 1966 when he told me the news." His orderly and painstaking planning for the Rio convention paid off. It was one of the best. "We were subject to change and uncertainty," wrote Luther in his trip report to his family and friends, "but we always came through." After strenuous side trips through Uruguay, Chile and other South American countries, Martha and Luther headed for home again. And in his final report of the 1948 South American journey, Luther waxed even more sentimental about homecoming. He said:

It has been a great experience, but we are happy to be home. I always feel that way about our America and about my state and town and family . . . This gratitude applies to simple things such as a good bed, a good mattress, a glass of pure cold water, a tomato you can trust, a cup of coffee served **when** you want it and as you want it. It also applies to things such as common understanding in language and mentality, to a confidence you are talking about the same thing and along the same lines. It means confidence in a transaction without wondering or worrying as to what the other guy is trying to do to you. It means a common faith in the greater good rather than strictly personal aggrandizement. It means pride in the future leadership and greatness of our country.

Betsy was married in 1946 to Donald Bernard, an engineer for an oil company, who lived in Washington, D.C. Nancy completed studies at an international diplomatic training school in Washington and accepted a job in Rangoon, Burma, where she met and fell in love with a British businessman, John C. Finlay. So it happened in May 1949 that Luther Hodges and Luther Hodges Jr., twelve years old, enplaned for Europe, the Middle East, India and Burma and beyond. Martha stayed at home. She made a later trip to Rangoon. In the 1949 travel, Luther Hodges' trip report was especially enlightening in that it reveals what he thought of his family, especially his only son. Luther Hodges is not a man to make a show of his emotions, and sometimes his children, especially his son, got the feeling that much was expected of them, that toeing the line was important, that excellence was expected in conduct and scholarship; but, on the other hand, praise was not the usual order of procedure. Therefore it was revealing to Luther Jr. to read in the trip report of 1949 what his father thought of him as a person. The father wrote:

> Luther Jr. has made the trip outstanding and I'd like to pay a tribute to him—he's the sweetest sanest twelve-year-old I've seen and everyone "around the world" felt the same way. He had judgment and balance, charm and intelligence, and by the time he was in Rangoon he was one of the best "bargainers" I've known . . . He's been good for me, has quieted and calmed me down many times and has been a most intelligent and helpful traveling companion.

They stopped first in London and drove through England, to Oxford, Eton, Windsor Castle, Runny-mede (where King John signed the Magna Charta). At Windsor, they saw Queen Elizabeth, Princess Elizabeth, and the Queen Mother Mary. Governor Luther Hodges reminded Queen Elizabeth years later at a football game in Virginia that he had once stood and watched her, as a Princess, pass by.

"Luther has had a chance to use some of his French on a short stop in Belgium," the father wrote in the trip report. "He's been a great sport on the whole trip and among other things has been handling money, making change and giving tips since we left New York." They flew to Beirut, Lebanon, to Damascus and on to Rangoon. Luther wrote, "It was wonderful to see Nancy. She and John Finlay met us at the airport." Luther Jr. lit the candles at the wedding ceremony, and Luther Sr. gave the bride away to John Finlay.

On the homeward journey, the two Luthers visited in Bangkok, Thailand, in Hong Kong, Okinawa and Japan. In the trip report is this entry:

> While we were sight-seeing (in Tokyo) I came to the conclusion that I would like for us to see General MacArthur and I mentioned it to Luther. He snickered and observed that such a thing wasn't possible. Then I had to do it!

They walked up to MacArthur's headquarters, asked for General MacArthur's office, took the elevator, were ushered through guards until they came to his outer office. A quizzical colonel came to see them, and Hodges said he wanted to thank General

MacArthur on behalf of all Americans. A moment later, the message came—"The General will see you."

Hodges writes:

MacArthur was magnificent and most friendly . . . We discussed Philippine politics. He's as dramatic as pictured . . . He was self-confident, almost cocky, but talked with ease, assurance and keen knowledge of the whole Far East, including China. He was very friendly with Luther Jr., since he has a son of his own who is 11.

The messages to his friends and family unfolds a new dimension in Luther Hodges, for he communicates some of the intimate thoughts that he doesn't say aloud in conversation and speeches, in the best "Dear Dairy" tradition. They also furnish an extra flavor to the hard work and tension that often accompanies high executive tasks. In a trip report, Luther tells of the meeting of the board of directors of Marshall Field and Company when he made a formal report on operations, inventory, production and profits and losses. Hughston MacBain, president of the corporation, presided, and Marshall Field III also was present. Directly in front of Luther Hodges was a director who wore a bow tie that lit up in brilliant colors when he touched a button in his pocket. "I find this most disconcerting," laughed Luther, and the episode helped them over the harder work of hearing about the inventories and other aspects of Marshall Field's business.

Campus scene at the University of North Carolina in Chapel Hill. Luther Hodges lived in Vance Dormitory his senior year at the university. Entrance to Vance is at center background. This is on Franklin Street. Rock wall surrounds campus as it existed in 1915-1919 period.

Chapter Nine

Rebuilding Western Europe

At mid-century Luther Hodges again changed the course of his life. In 1950 he retired from Marshall Field and Company and accepted a proferred challenge in national and international service to help build up the economy of Western Europe. After this task was completed in 1951 he went into politics in North Carolina, winning the post of Lieutenant Governor in 1952 and then succeeding to the Governorship upon the death of the incumbent governor in 1954.

Although retirement from Marshall Field must have been a major break from the 31 years of strictly business and sales and industrial production, with its myriad pressures and successes, Luther Hodges announced his decision with the same calmness and definite purposefulness that was typical of the man. At 52 he was ready to try something else. He was not a wealthy man, but had saved enough to live moderately without salary income. He owned stock in Howard Johnson Restaurants, a lumber company, an oil distributorship, real estate, and a number of nationally-known corporations. He had tasted the fruits of national and world service, through the United States government, Rotary International assignments and United Nations observation-consultation. As one who always stopped from time to time and assessed his personal situation—for setting priorities on his interests, his time, and his future—Luther Hodges chose to retire from active business and devote the rest of his life to public service.

People of North Carolina read in their newspapers that Luther H. Hodges had transferred his headquarters from New York back to Leaksville, North Carolina. Tar Heels then heard on April 1950, that he had retired. A short time later, they learned that Robert M. Hanes, former president of the American Bankers Association and Chairman of the Board of Wachovia Bank & Trust Company in Winston Salem, North Carolina (the largest bank between Washington and Atlanta), had persuaded Luther Hodges to join him in his Marshall Plan work in Western Germany. The President of the United States picked Hanes as Chief of Mission in the Economic Cooperation Administration. The ECA would be the vehicle for putting West Germany back on its feet economically and for permiting the conquered nation to be a useful partner of other European countries rather than be an economic drag on the rest of the world. General George C. Marshall had made his famous speech at Harvard University, espousing economic aid in building up Europe which had been devastated by war. Luther Hodges was excited about the potentialities of the Marshall Plan. He accepted Robert Hanes' invitation to international service. He was chief of ECA's Industry Division. His goal: to help restore West German industry so that it would be self-supporting, money-making, profit realizing, and an essential cog in the trading between European nations and the world. This called for getting skilled Germans back on jobs, retraining people in new skills, restoring lost industry and starting new.

He tackled his new duties with his usual verve and insight and driving energy. In fact, he worked so hard that several times in the months of his negotiations with Germans, British, French, Americans and others of Europe and the world that Robert Hanes insisted Luther halt his work at times, for occasional vacations. These he took in Austria, in Germany, in Switzerland and other places—hunting, fishing, seeing the sights. Then it was back to work again on reconstruction of the defeated nation.

Martha and Luther Jr. went with him to Germany, young Luther attending high school in Germany. Their West German home was in Frankfurt with offices in Frankfurt, Bremen, Wiesbaden, Stuttgart, Munich and West Berlin.

All was not easy sailing in the rebuilding of West Germany, nor had Luther expected it would be. Re-employing Germans and getting their industry built up and unlimbered had to be accompanied by promoting cooperation between former enemies who had to become economic allies if all were to achieve maximum recovery. There were those who thought

German Industrial potential should be destroyed and the nation made mainly agrarian. That was uneconomic, not only for the industrially-skilled Germans, but for the rest of the world as well. The notion of keeping Germany destitute was rejected. But the cooperative spirit was not easy to evoke. Hodges told of his early conferences with British and French representatives on ECA. "I was anxious to talk with them as to their ideas on lifting the restrictions on German steel production," he wrote to friends. "I was somewhat disheartened to find out two things, which I probably already knew: the British subordinate everything to 'commercial competition' and the French, in turn, subordinate everything to their own 'security.' These attitudes seriously affect progress—and the Americans, with their ideals of what ought to be done for the good of the world, have become quite impatient with their allies for not facing up to the critical situation which now exists." He confided in his trip report of August 16, 1950:

> We are right now in a struggle at the top levels with the British and French to get them to help us with the Berlin situation—our show place. . . . The British and French are living in splendor such as they haven't known before and are exploiting their colonial efforts to the limit. One of the high Britishers has 30-40 servants, all charged to occupation costs.

Hodges took a tough tone with the British and French. On a discussion on West German steel development, he said of obstacles placed in his path:

"By that time I was pretty roused up and talked to them pretty frankly."

Hodges felt, in appraising Germany's recovery, it was important to recollect that early in 1948 economic conditions in that country were a threat to free governments everywhere. But by 1950 there was ample evidence that West Germany and Western Europe had progressed far enough economically to resist what Luther called "alien pressures from within"—that is, Communism. There was also evidence that the growing economic strength would prove to be a sound foundation to support whatever defensive measures were needed to deter aggression from Russia. "Today it is clear that the need for economic strength has never been greater," Hodges declared in a speech to West Germans in Wiesbaden in 1950. "Without a strong Western Europe the peace of the world is in danger." Hodges held that it wasn't simply a story of German recovery, but a story of Marshall Plan countries working together toward a common goal—free nations working as one for the recovery of all.

He was able to say later, when recovery was in high gear:

The situation in Germany from a business standpoint in the last few weeks has reached a position about as fantastic as what we have heard from the States. The rate of industrial production in the month of September jumped 114 percent (counting 1936 production as 100 percent) and in August to 121 percent.

Hodges was also delighted to report that "Businessmen are coming into the office by the dozens asking to make contacts with German firms in order to buy goods."

Hodges worked with many people who later were prominent in international life, among them High Commissioner for West Germany, John J. McCloy, who became head of the Chase National Bank and Ludwig Erhard, later president of West Germany. On one occasion Hodges was a spectator at a press conference when correspondents interviewed the United States Military Chief, General Lucius Clay. He said of Clay: "His mind is very quick, and he answered questions by the time they were out of the questioner's mouth." A Rotary advisor on public relations and himself a good man as the principal figure at a press conference, Luther Hodges seemed to admire in General Clay a proficiency in which Hodges also excelled.

Luther Jr. made top grades in school, played basketball and went hunting for wild boar with his father. On one hunt, the 14-year-old Hodges hit a deer at 200 yards, using a German Mauser rifle with a telescopic sight.

At the busy Frankfurt railroad station one evening, Martha had her pocket picked. They reconstructed what had happened and remembered that a short stranger had brushed Luther Jr. aside to get next to Martha. The man had taken her purse from her pocketbook, which contained not only money but also her diplomatic passport, ration card, commissionery card, driver's licenses (North Carolina and Germany). The next day Martha received her passport through the mail. The pickpocket kept the rest. Luther assured her the valuables were covered by insurance and the missing documents could be reissued.

One day they received a telegram from Rangoon, Burma. Nancy had given birth to identical twin girls! The normally calm Luther and almost-as-imperturbable Luther Jr., were excited. It was Martha's turn to be stoical. She said matter-of-factly, "I suppose that means double the number of diapers we had expected."

Just as Luther's gigantic task in West Germany was over, he was invited to take on a similar job in Italy, but he declined. He was ready to go home. However, he did accept a U. S. State Department call to serve as a consultant for the International Management Conference. He helped in the organization of the conference, inviting about 100 top European industrialists and businessmen to visit the United States and see the latest techniques in management and manufacturing. They toured the country; it was a fitting climax to the fruitful groundwork and constructive service in Europe and tied the United States even closer with Western Europe.

Back in Leaksville, he was attending to his personal business matters when one day he received a phone call from B. Everett Jordan, long-time friend, fellow lay leader in the Methodist Church, Rotarian, and colleague in the textile business. The whole Jordan family of Saxapahaw have long been prominent in North Carolina industry, education, law, politics, and civic and religious life. (Jordan is now U. S. Senator from North Carolina).

"Luther, you ought to run for Lieutenant Governor," said Jordan.

"Not me" said Luther almost involuntarily.

Jordan continued, "I want you to consider this seriously. Do you remember in your speeches when you told us that businessmen ought to be in government? It's **your** theory. I think it's a good one. You ought to practice what you preach," he said.

"I'll think it over," promised Hodges.

For the next two weeks he consulted other people. These included, he later wrote, "friends, friend-politicians, and politicians." In most cases they told him he should run. Some reserved judgment and others said, "I'll let you know," and never did.

He looked at the opposition for the Democratic primary. His main opponent would be Roy Rowe, an experienced legislator in the state from Burgaw in Pender County. Rowe had the support of most politicians in the state—as well as the lobbyists. Another candidate was Marshall Kurfees, mayor of Winston-Salem; a third was Ben J. McDonald of Wilmington.

At the end of two weeks he had made his decision. Yes, he would run.

Unlike the practice in some states and in the national government in which the governor and lieutenant governor run on the same ticket as the president and vice president run jointly in the national political conventions, North Carolina has a system whereby candidates for governor run apart from the candidates for lieutenant governor. The candidate for governor was William B. Umstead, also a graduate of the University of North Carolina and former United States Senator appointed to fill the unexpired term of Senator J. W. Bailey who had died in office. Umstead was defeated in running for his first full term as senator; the victor was J. M. Broughton of Raleigh, former governor. In the Broughton-Umstead Senatorial election, Luther Hodges had lent his support to Broughton. But this didn't matter greatly as he was running separately rather than on the same ticket with Umstead.

Early in 1952, Martha and Luther Hodges drove to Raleigh for politicking at the Democratic Party's annual Jefferson-Jackson Day Dinner. It was the occasion for top political leaders and the grassroots workers to gather. It was a good place for Hodges to be—to size up who was for him and against him. Lyndon B. Johnson once said, "If a man can't walk into a room full of people and in just a few minutes find out which ones are for him and which ones are against him, he has no business in politics." At that political dinner in Raleigh in 1952 Luther Hodges didn't know, **at first**, who was for him and against him. Luther seemed to feel good about the courtesies shown him. But he had someone at his side, Martha Hodges, who has an intuitive sense about such things. She apprised Luther of what she believed to be which way the political wind was blowing. "Those people are not for you," she told Luther. Editor Jonathan Daniels said in the Raleigh **News and Observer:** "Hodges made a good impression, but the crowd was for Rowe." Said Luther Hodges, "That about sums it up."

Hodges called on some of his friends in large North Carolina corporations. They, too, were friendly. But many had made commitments to others. The bleak prospect caused Luther Hodges to be all the more determined to win. He took his case to the people. Driving in an old Buick, he stopped frequently at service stations bought a dollars' worth of gas at a time. He introduced himself and talked with the people.

In the western part of the state, Luther drove into the mountain town of Andrews and called on a banker friend, Percy Ferebee.

Ferebee said frankly, "We're all for Rowe up here and we will elect him."

"Well," said Hodges, "is there any use of my spending my time in the town of Andrews?"

"None whatsoever," replied Ferebee.

On his way out of Andrews, Luther said to Bill Shope of Weaverville, who was for him and was showing him through the mountain counties, "I just don't believe there's anybody that good. I couldn't be and I don't think you could be and I don't think Mr. Ferebee can be. Why don't we stop at this filling station?"

Hodges asked the filling station man about his view of Hodges' chances, and he told him what Percy Ferebee had said.

"Mr. Ferebee is not speaking for all of us," said the man.

Luther asked, "Who is the man I should see to get some help?"

He said, "Chunk Love."

"Where do you find Chunk Love?" asked the candidate.

He pointed to a house where a man was standing on the roof fixing shingles and said, "That's Chunk."

Chunk Love was cooperative from the start. "I'll be glad to do whatever I can," he said.

Hodges remembers, "We came out all right in Andrews."

At first Luther found it embarrassing to ask a man for his vote. Luther Hodges' basic policy of refusing to be "beholden" to anybody or to obligate himself for any reason whatsoever seemed to be adverse to his new role of political candidate. Luther steeled himself again, and as he paid his check going out of a cafe in Goldsboro, he said to the lady cashier, "I'm Luther Hodges. I'm a candidate for lieutenant governor. I would appreciate your support." Without waiting for a reply, he jammed his hat on his head and walked away. The cashier called after him, "I'm for you, if you haven't ever been to Washington or to Raleigh before." After that it was easier. Following the first jump into cold political waters, Luther became less bashful. He would say his spiel and hasten to the next prospective voter. The salesman in him burst forth. He was offering them his services! He got into the swing of campaigning and enjoyed it.

Contributors to his campaign, a matter of public record, were all Leaksville people: Ben C. Trotter, $500; Harold Whitcomb of Marshall Field, $500; H.

F. Fitchett, $750; Mrs. Luther Hodges, $1,500; and Luther Hodges himself, $3,937.03, for a total campaign budget of $7,212.03. Hodges adhered to a policy of "no villification; no mudslinging; no name-calling." He made no promises, no commitments. "I didn't know what I could deliver," he said. "I wasn't going to promise anything I couldn't deliver." His message: good government and business-type efficiency in government.

Luther won the primary election in May. He was far ahead of both opposing candidates. His lead over the nearest opponent, Rowe, was 70,000 votes. The vote was Hodges, 226,167; Rowe, 151,067; Kurfees, 55,055; McDonald, 52,916. Luther didn't have the necessary majority and there was likelihood of a runoff between Hodges and Rowe. However, Rowe didn't ask for a runoff. In the November elections, Democrat Hodges beat Republican Warren H. Pritchett of Spruce Pine by a vote of 783,792 to 374,530.

Following his succcessful election, a **Greensboro Daily News** political reporter wrote:

He is a tall man who walks with a slight purposeful stoop as if leaning forward a little to get where he's going with utmost dispatch . . . He moves quietly, smoothly and directly with a kind of loose-jointed grace and he speaks with a smooth but earnest determination in his tone.

His face reflects a mixture of strength and shyness, possessing heavy dark eyebrows in contrast of his white hair; bright, lively eyes; a firmly-modeled nose; a rather large mobile mouth. His manner, friendly but resolute, is that of a man accustomed to getting things done with the least fuss and bother.

After his election and before he took office, Hodges prepared for his many responsibilities. He went back to school—to Chapel Hill. Albert Coates, who was a sophomore when Luther was a freshman and who had noticed the overpowering vigor of the youngster from Leaksville's mills, had become a professor of criminal law in the university and had founded a law-enforcement and government-studies institute that was unique in the United States. The Institute of Government is an unusual kind of adult-education school. Professor Coates had found during the 1920's, when Hodges was rising in Marshall Field and Company, that there was a gap that should be bridged between what faculty taught students in law school and what is actually practiced in government. The vacancy between theory and practice as these affect public servants in city halls and county court houses, and in the State Capitol, was formidable. In classes at Chapel Hill, public servants learned from professors. In turn, professors heard how law enforcement actually works in the 100 counties of North Carolina. They swapped views. The Institute of Government taught "how to do it." Among students enrolling for the expanding Institute of Government of the University of North Carolina were clerks of court, registrars of deeds, judges, city managers, sheriffs, police, highway patrolmen, jailers, city planners and zoners, tax collectors, members of the Legislature, prosecuting attorneys, juvenile court judges—and now the Lieutenant Governor-elect, Luther H. Hodges. He was the only one in his class, and he studied the duties of his office which included presiding over the Senate.

In an interview Lieutenant Governor Hodges later cited what he considered the advantages and the disadvantages of a businessman in government. The disadvantages:

1. A businessman is usually too inclined to rush in and be abrupt.

2. He fails to realize things are done by a series of compromises.

3. Most businessmen have a communications gap to overcome in their talk to the public.

4. Most business men don't like to ask favors.

But here are the advantages:

1. Businessmen are usually good organizers and administrators.

2. They generally have a direct, honest approach in politics, which is appealing to voters.

3. A business man is independent and not tied down by strings or commitments.

4. Bureaucrats get recognition by the number of people they boss and how much money they spend. Businessmen get ahead by just the opposite—the more they trim in waste and deadwood, the more they're worth to their company.

In a speech to North Carolinians, Hodges spoke of the deplorable payola type gifts by industrialists to executives in government in return for favors. He scorned certain scandals in Washington involving what he considered unethical conduct. Hodges said, "Nobody has a monopoly on corruption and dishonesty, or on honesty. Behind every mink coat there is a mink coat giver. Behind every collector there is a crooked taxpayer."

One North Carolina editor spoke gleefully about the dismay of lobbyists at Luther Hodges' approaching tenure, and at the realization that they had not supported him in the primary. The newspaperman wrote:

> Lobbyists are worried. They are worried about Luther Hodges whom most of them opposed vigorously.
>
> They are trying to butter him up.
>
> They know a strong Lieutenant Governor has more influence with regard to controversial legislation than the Governor himself.
>
> Luther Hodges is the strongest Lieutenant Governor North Carolina has had in years.
>
> And the smartest.
>
> He beat the lobbyists and the Old Guard politicians.

North Carolina had a new powerful man high in public life, a gentleman of business acumen, a man of the people who had made good, who had performed important tasks well on the national and international scene, and whose interests seemed to be for the good of the people and were approached in a businesslike manner. The people liked him. They, not the politicians, had put him in office. In an agricultural state turning into a moderately industrial economy to give more balance, thousands of farmers were migrating from farm to factory, from country to town. Knowing this was the thing Luther Hodges and his family had done successfully in accomplishing "The American Dream," the people of North Carolina "identified with him" in the dramatic and literary terminology. Luther Hodges was a genuine folk hero. Harold Whitcomb of Marshall Field thought there was at least one other thing going in Hodges' favor. It was Rotary. "Rotary is a non-political organization," said Whitcomb, "and Rotary is not used in favor of any candidate. But Luther Hodges was well known all over the state in Rotary circles, and that meant he had a number of people who were certainly favorably disposed toward him, people who were civic and community leaders of the state."

Chapter Ten

Governor of North Carolina

Everywhere he went in North Carolina Luther Hodges saw his picture staring at him from telephone poles.

During his campaign he viewed his picture on billboards, in store windows, on posts and sides of barns with something approaching shock. "They are littering up the countryside," Luther thought to himself, and there was a tinge of chagrin in his orderly nature that the "Vote for Hodges" signs were contributing to what he thought was a mess on the highway landscape. It especially irked him to see the posters nailed to trees. When he complained to his campaign managers, he was assured that everyone else did it. In self-defense Hodges would have to do it, too.

When the election was over, Luther Hodges continued to run up against his picture on the highways, and he resolved to do something about it. He paid a team of men to ride around the state and take down many of the campaign signs. He telephoned volunteers in several parts of the state and asked them to see that the posters were removed. "It was effectively done and I felt better," said the Lieutenant Governor. The act caused ripples of favorable editorial comment in the press.

Governor Umstead was inaugurated January 13, 1953, and Luther Hodges was sworn in as Lieutenant Governor on the same occasion. It was a jam-packed day. After the inaugural ceremonies and speeches, parades, dinner, reception and handshaking—all day long—there was the concluding event, the Inaugural Ball.

Over 4,000 North Carolinians lined up to shake the hands of the Governor and the Lieutenant Governor. One by one the hands were pumped, and some of the shakes were vigorous, finger-compressing and knuckle-bruising. Luther later described the political handclasps as—"crushing." The two election victors were wearied. At one point Governor Umstead turned to Hodges and said with a grimace, "My right leg is hurting me."

Later, at the ball, Governor Umstead was urged to play the harmonica. He was very good at folk tunes. On this occasion he declined at first. But the audience, mistaking his attitude for modesty, insisted. He finally played. "The crowd enjoyed it, but I could tell Governor Umstead was tired," said Luther, "and that he was in no mood for even being up, much less playing the harmonica. He was then a sick man." In retrospect Luther referred to the tight schedule of that inauguration day as "somewhat barbaric."

The next night Governor Umstead was stricken. For the next 22 months, Governor Umstead was in and out of the hospital. But even in his critical condition Umstead carried on the work of the Governor. He insisted upon it.

Lieutenant Governor Hodges presided over the State Senate, one of the major assignments of his office. Just before the General Assembly of 1953 was to begin, Luther was stopped in the lobby of the Hotel Sir Walter by a man who was an experienced lobbyist.

The lobbyist said, "Let's you and I take a bottle of Scotch and go up to my room and set up your Senate committees."

The astonished Hodges said, "Will you repeat that?"

The man said it again. He added, "I've helped before on matters like this."

"Well, this is where it stops," said Hodges. "No one is going to make my appointments but me."

Luther studied the names and personal histories of each senator before he made his committee appointments. He found out what part of the state they came from, the interests of each man, the assignments they had held on previous committees. "I feel we should not appoint a legislator to a committee because of the influence of the people who have a personal or corporate interest in it." Only Luther Hodges knew whom he would name. When the day came for the appointments he distributed the list to the Senators at the same time he gave it to the press.

The lieutenant governor does not vote except in case of a tie. A tie happened only once in 1953. A bill was introduced requiring the withdrawal of a driver's license if he were caught speeding over seventy miles an hour. Hodges voted **for** the law.

On his first day as presiding officer of the Senate, Luther stopped at a flower shop on his way to the State Capitol building. On an impulse he bought a white carnation. "I need it for my spirits," he said. The white carnation became a trademark for Luther Hodges, and North Carolinians from 1954 to 1960 seldom if ever saw him without a white carnation in his lapel.

When the Number Two Man becomes the Number One Man, what goes on in his mind? What does he think of his succession? What is he going to do with the office and responsibilities he now must undertake? What is his attitude towards his predecessor who has died in office? What does the Vice President think about when the President is sick? In the cases of Lincoln, Franklin D. Roosevelt, and John F. Kennedy, what were the special personal composure problems confronting their Vice Presidents when these Presidents fell? Historians as well as commentators on the spot often feel impelled to deal with these grisly details. To the credit of Andrew Johnson, Harry Truman and Lyndon Johnson, these trying events were met with poise. Such dignity was likewise the manner of Luther H. Hodges when Governor William B. Umstead died and Hodges took his place. Although it was apparent to the people of the state that Governor Umstead was in danger for over a year and a half after he took office, there was in the North Carolina press a relative absence of conjecture about a possible succession. In national politics, the columnists under such circumstances would unquestionably be devoting reams to speculation, and so would the television interpreters of news. Their editors would demand it. If legislators and others in Raleigh talked about it, they were discreet. The issue didn't come up in conferences. Certainly Luther Hodges didn't discuss it. Although he had from his childhood steeled himself to be "prepared" for whatever obligation he might be called upon to fulfill—even to the extent of taking a Sunday School teacher's place in the lesson if that person should falter—Hodges had not let the idea that he would become Governor dwell in his mind. Yes, he had **thought** of it! During Governor Umstead's prolonged illness, the thought had occasionally flashed through Luther Hodges' mind. But he didn't let the notion stay there. "I made no plans, no decisions, and I had no practical reaction." Luther Hodges kept his poise during those tense 22 months. He did his job. As usual he threw himself wholly into his work.

The same calmness was sustained when on November 7, 1954, he was phoned at his home in Leaksville and notified that Governor Umstead had died. Ed Rankin, private secretary to Governor Umstead was calling. "Governor Hodges," he said, "Governor Umstead died a little after nine o'clock this morning."

Luther Hodges was stunned. He sat in his chair a few moments without rising. "For a while I prayed there in that chair," he said. Then Martha and Luther went to church as they had planned for that Sunday morning.

The lack of planning and anticipation for the succession was immediately encountered. Hodges telephoned North Carolina's Secretary of State Thad Eure to ask about the procedure to be followed. There was also a question of title. Was Luther Hodges already Governor of North Carolina? Did he have to wait to be sworn in to become Governor? When would that be?

Eure had some surprising news. He said he questioned whether Hodges could be called Governor even after he was sworn in. Hodges title would be Acting Governor, said Eure.

"As a matter of common sense it did not seem practical for the state to have only an acting governor," said Luther. He telephoned the chief justice of the North Carolina Supreme Court, Maurice Victor Barnhill. Judge Barnhill said that Luther Hodges' title was Governor, that he should be sworn in—but agreed with Luther that it was proper to wait until after Governor Umstead's funeral before taking the oath of office. This oath was taken November 9, 1954 in the Capitol's Hall of the House of Representatives. "As I took the oath of office, I determined with God's help to serve North Carolina and its people to the best of my ability," said Governor Hodges.

He went to work on Wednesday, November 10, and the first man he saw was Ed Rankin. Ed was a former newspaperman, a graduate of the University of North Carolina, later a public relations man, and had served as private secretary to Umstead when he was a United States Senator and during Umstead's 22 months as governor.

"Let's sit down and talk," said Hodges.

"I know that the governor may wish to have his own man as his secretary," began Rankin. "I can wind up my things in a few days. Or I can be ready to make the change tomorrow. I am at your service, and I want to do what you'd like me to do."

"I know it's customary to change some personnel," said the governor, "but my case is different. I'm new to this office, did not run for it, and have no obligations to pay off to anyone. I'd like you to stay a while, and we'll see how it works out."

So Rankin sat tight. In about two weeks, Hodges said one day, "Everything is going fine." Rankin stayed with Hodges the next five years.

After Ed left that first day, Governor Hodges noticed a row of buttons on his desk. Since he didn't know what button was for what person, he pushed the first one. It was a way of saying "hello" and getting acquainted and finding out what each person did. He pushed all the buttons and asked, "What do you do?" Then he asked each of them why they did it the way they described. Most of the answers were, "It has always been done that way."

Just as the button-pushing episode was over, a secretary brought in a paper. "Governor, please sign this," she said.

"Sign what?" asked Governor Hodges.

"Sign this paper," she said.

"What's it for?" asked the governor.

"Your signature on this paper will simply indicate that you are on the payroll as governor," said the secretary, "and that your money will be sent to you at the end of the month."

"This is not the army!" said Governor Hodges. "I'm not going to sign any payroll. They have a record of when I came. I see no reason for my signing it."

"You won't sign it?" said the secretary.

"No," said the governor. "Not until I get a good reason for signing it."

The secretary presented her problem to Ed Rankin. Ed called the attorney general for an opinion.

"No, he doesn't have to sign," said the attorney general. "Now that someone is questioning it, I can say this practice has been going on for a 100 years and is completely unnecessary."

Luther knew it was only a tiny matter, but it represented wasted motion. The lesson also bore out a pet Hodges theory: that the principles of good business could and should apply in government. The incident over the pay voucher, though minor, was Governor Hodges' first effort to make the state government of North Carolina more efficient and more economical. It was the beginning of many efficiency innovations in Hodges' reorganization. "I had learned through experience, when a problem presented itself, to: inquire into it, size it up, and then make a definite decision," he said. Governor Hodges immediately began to delegate responsibility. He created some excitement in his office by telling people to take over and complete jobs—and at the same time be held responsible for their proper execution. He asked department directors in Raleigh: "What are your plans for the future? What will be your needs and programs for the next ten years? Many of them must have thought the request was crazy, but they came through with the reports," said the governor. "These reports gave us some idea of how things might grow and what might be needed."

Hodges took office just two months before the General Assembly met for its biennial session. An important preparatory task is presenting a budget for the next two years to run all the operations of North Carolina's government. He met with the state's Advisory Budget Commission and found that the amount of money requested from the state agencies far exceeded what was expected from revenues anticipated. The difference of what was wanted over what was to be expected amounted to $52 million for the two years. The heavy demand came for vital state services—mental institutions, highways, education, agriculture, welfare, conservation and development, and others.

It looked as though Governor Hodges would either have to deny requests considered just, or would have to ask for a raise in taxes. He considered a sales tax and rejected the notion. In his message to the General Assembly, he advocated an excise tax on tobacco products, soft drinks and spiritous liquors.

Tobacco is one of North Carolina's main industries. Previous efforts to impose a tobacco tax in North Carolina had been defeated. "We are not unmindful of the importance of our tobacco growing and manufacturing industries in this state," said Governor Hodges. "However, information obtained from reliable sources discloses that other states which have in recent years imposed excise taxes on tobacco products have not experienced any appreciable decline in the consumption of such products."

Later in his book, **Businessman in the Statehouse,** Hodges wrote: "Opponents to my proposed tax felt that if North Carolina, the prime tobacco state, put a tax on the product, then other states would do likewise. This argument did not hold water, but it was hard to even deny it. At that time forty-one of the forty-eight states and the District of Columbia imposed consumer taxes on tobacco products. Other states have since levied taxes on tobacco products, but North Carolina has not."

The battle of the budget raged for several weeks. Finally the situation was relieved by what is called an "improved revenue outlook." It looked as though North Carolina was going to get more from normal taxation. It was like finding money in the mattress that you had forgotten was there. When the budget of $640 million was adopted, the largest one in North Carolina history up to that time, the new taxes were primarily on beer and wine.

Ed Rankin knows better than most people Luther Hodges' ability to communicate. "He discussed everything with me—about office and governmental matters," Rankin said. "He didn't hold back. We had no secrets between us. He was a great delegator; he gave sufficient information; he let you do the job. But he made sure the job was done."

Rankin was stimulated by the fast pace that Hodges set. "Governor Hodges is a ball of fire and a volcano of physical energy," said his secretary. "He never took a coffee break, stopped only briefly for a light lunch, worked straight on through until the end of the day."

Rankin kept a wooden, mahogany-colored box, two-by-three feet, with brass handles in which the governor kept his mail. The mail box was transported everywhere Hodges went, and he'd read his mail—except that which Rankin had withheld as routine and could be answered by others. The governor carried an electric recorder and dictated letters and memoranda. "He seldom dictated in the office," said Rankin. "That was done at nights at home, and he'd bring in disks for transcribing the first thing every morning."

His office appointments lasted about fifteen minutes at the most. If the conversation was going on too long, the governor had ways of halting it. "He would jiggle coins or rise, and the guest would have to rise with him," said Ed. "He wouldn't waste time in circumlocution. He went straight to the heart of a matter in any conference." When an interview with a bureaucrat became extended and nebulous, the governor invariably broke in and would suggest something like: "Well, what we're really driving at is this, isn't it?"

Ed Rankin wrote many of Hodges' speeches. "I drafted the speeches at first, and he made changes. As in other ghost-writing tasks, I finally fell into the way he liked to say things and could organize facts and put them in language in the way he wanted it expressed." Speech research was handled by a girl in the office, and Rankin based much of the speech forms on that research. Later in the Hodges' administration, an additional speech writer was hired to assist.

Governor Hodges' greatest contribution to the state has been the campaign for new industry, Rankin feels. "Raising the state's per capita income was his first and most important goal, and bringing in new industry and starting new home-grown business were the ways of going about it," said his secretary. "Governor Hodges had the contacts. He would pick up the phone and call Tom Watson of IBM or call the president of Union Carbide—they were old friends and talked the same business language."

Ed Rankin found his new boss complex. The principles of independence and refusing to exert influence to friends and relatives are basic with the man, "a part of the dominating spirit of his life," said Rankin. "He would do no favor for you if it were not in accord with his principles. However, he would do personal favors, and he did this in secret. Very few people know anything about this part of his character."

"He is impatient, has a temper, is impulsive and is infinitely skilled in grasping facts quickly. He was so quick himself he would sometimes become infuriated by slow-thinking when he ran up against it."

The story of Luther Hodges, from boyhood to manhood, is indeed a Horatio Alger classic, in Rankin's opinion.

Luther Hodges when he was Vice President and General Manager of Marshall Field and Co. (About 1951.)

Chapter Eleven

Picking a Team

Governor Luther Hodges needed an aide, a man with legal knowledge. He reached out again to the Institute of Government at Chapel Hill and invited Paul Johnston to call on him. Johnston was a Law School graduate of the university and an assistant director of Albert Coates' Institute of Government. Johnston's main field was administrative law, but he had also performed research for a committee appointed by Governor Umstead on "Reorganization of State Government."

"I had never met Governor Hodges prior to that day," said Johnston. "I was strictly nonpolitical. I had never even been in the State Capitol before. Politics was an abstraction to me. I had no root connections in practical political affars."

These drawbacks were explained by Johnston to the governor, but Hodges said that it didn't matter. He was a little suspicious of people with political backgrounds anyhow.

"I'm not even sure whether I voted for you for lieutenant governor," Johnston said to Hodges.

Hodges brushed that aside, too. He asked Johnston to go to work immediately. Instead of resigning from the Institute of Government, Johnston took a six months leave of absence. "I had no desire to be in politics," he said. But after only a few weeks with Governor Hodges, Johnston made up his mind to stay "for the duration." "I was intrigued and fascinated," he said. "I knew I would stay."

The day of Johnston's appointment as Hodges' chief aid, members of the press asked the governor, "Is Paul Johnston a Democrat or a Republican."

"Omigod," said the governor, "I forgot to ask him."

One of the backlogs of work facing Governor Hodges was a list of a thousand overdue appointments. Governor Hodges called on Paul Johnston and Ed Rankin to help him study the jobs and the people to occupy them. "My first job was to look up the law and submit a memorandum on holdovers," said Johnston. "We had to examine the qualifications of candidates, or others available, and look into the requirements of the offices. We had to take note of the geographical area the prospects came from. We made an estimate of the preferred background of a potential office holder."

Information was provided about each job and each man recommended for the post.

Paul Johnston found government service in Raleigh stimulating and excting. His capacity for organization and hard work and implementation of

Luther and Martha Hodges at a dinner for the Governor of North Carolina in Greensboro, August 1955.

decisions was respected by Governor Hodges, and the governor in turn gave Johnston even greater responsibilities. The governor organized a Department of Administration and put Johnston at the head of it. This gave Johnston a purview over the fiscal and operating management of all state agencies.

Martha and Luther lived in a large mansion a few blocks from the Capitol. Their home was a center of social activity for the city and the state, and it was also a focal point for protocol and extra-governmental ceremonials in which Martha Hodges played a gracious role.

Luther Hodges Jr. was eighteen years old and a sophomore at the university in Chapel Hill. He spent many weekends with his mother and father; he was active in campus student self-government at the university—and as usual (and expected by his father) an excellent scholar. There were special occasions when Betsy Hodges Bernard and her husband and their children came to visit. Nancy and John Finlay and their children came from Burma. These were memorable occasions for the Hodges family, even though it was not all private, but subjected to the glare of publicity that goes with the governorship. Luther's family from Leaksville and Spray came to dinners and receptions, too.

Although Luther Hodges had been strict at Marshall Field in avoiding nepotism or any suspicion of it, just as he stayed at arm's length from any odor of favoritism in government, he was always willing and ready to help friends and family in a personal way. Christmas time was the time for gifts—and the sisters each received a check for $100.

Betsy Bernard, in addition to a regular gift each Christmas, could expect from her father two other remembrances—Halo Shampoo and a can of shrimp, reminiscent of a family joke between them.

In the summer the Hodges family vacationed at the beach and in the mountains of North Carolina.

Luther Hodges called North Carolina's major hurdle a "bread and butter problem." People demanded services; they wanted and deserved in midcentury America the good things of life. But North Carolinians did not have the income, per capita, to support what they wanted. After a survey in which he found that North Carolina was ranked 44th in the nation in per capita wealth, Governor Hodges investigated the reasons why.

First, he asked President Gordon Gray of the University of North Carolina to survey the facts. Governor Hodges wondered if it could be so, that North Carolina was 44th among the 48 states in per capita wealth. President Gray found out. Yes, it was true. North Carolina's income per person was behind the per capita incomes of 43 other states of the union.

Except for ten counties in the industrial Piedmont region of North Carolina, most of the rest of the state was agricultural. There were industries in the east and in the far west, but these were chiefly low-paying industries. There was the problem of farm unemployment, mechanization resulting from the people's leaving the land to go to work in the towns where mills hired plenty of labor for low wages.

The solution was to bring in new industry, the kind of industry that paid higher wages. Luther wrote:

Industralization, with all of its advantages to the people and to the state, became the number one goal of my administration. I began at once the long and intensive campaign to acquaint the people of the state with the actual situation of North Carolina and its relation with the other forty-seven states and to point out that we had to raise the per capita income if we were to raise the standard of living of our people. One of the best means of achieving this was more local industries, more small factories, and more processing plants for converting the state's raw materials into greater income-yielding products. This would also give work and wages to our underemployed. It would give opportunity for our trained specialists and a broad base for taxation from which we could get revenue to carry on the needed services for our people.

When he was lieutenant governor, Hodges had attended one of several meetings of the Department of Conservation and Development. The particular agenda and purpose was to tell communities how to get ready for new industry. Hodges gives credit to Umstead for his foresight. "Such meetings led me to believe that had Governor Umstead lived and kept his health he would have done a good job in the area of industrialization," said Hodges.

The governor looked over available men to become head of the Conservation and Development

Department, a post vacated by Ben Douglas of Charlotte. Then he telephoned William P. Saunders, retired from the textile business and living in Southern Pines. Saunders and Hodges had known each other at Chapel Hill. They had remained in touch in the textile business, and Hodges knew that Saunders had many national contacts. He also knew that Saunders knew how to run a big organization and was adept in administration and how to deal with people.

He said to Saunders, "Bill, are you tired of fishing and resting?"

"Yes, I am," said Saunders.

"We want you to come to Raleigh and head up the Department of Conservation and Development. We want to put North Carolina in the forefront of industry."

Saunders agreed to do it, and for the next five years they worked together building up an industry-seeking organization. The practice of "wooing and winning" industry from one state and one region to another has been going on a long time, but the refinements made by Luther Hodges in North Carolina are distinctive. It was not only a pitch to large industries to move entirely to North Carolina, nor to expand their national operations when new regional plants were established. It was more than that. Hodges first wanted to sow seeds for home-grown industry in the state, to foster little businesses, ventures that would grow to bigger ones later. "We will have to pull ourselves up by our own bootstraps," said the governor. The main obstacle was credit. Based on studies by Capus Waynick, a successful "Point Four" leader under President Truman, it was practicable to propose to the 1955 Legislature that a credit or development corporation be formed to lend money. Long-term capital would be furnished to individuals and groups to start small businesses or expand existing businesses. The Legislature approved, and Waynick went about raising money by selling stock. Governor Hodges bought the first $1,000 worth of stock, and he later bought $4,000 more. Waynick then urged the governor to personally get in on the act of salesmanship. This was a challenge to salesman Hodges and he didn't resist it. "I felt that various groups such as bus lines, motor trucks, railroads and utilities ought to be in the middle of the campaign since they would benefit quickly," said Hodges. He wanted to get a large purchase of stock—as an example for other firms— so he went to Duke Power Company, and at first was turned down. But he didn't give up. He approached it from another direction, tried Duke Power again and sold $100,000 worth of stock. Other firms came in. Finally, North Carolina Business Development Corporation was a reality, with $1 million in stock. Then they canvassed banks and other financial institutions, asking them to make money available on call to the Development Corporation based on a certain percentage of the capital and reserves. With the original million dollars in stock and the participation of bankers and insurance companies, the "Operation Bootstraps" was going well.

"All over North Carolina there began to rise up small companies," wrote Hodges. These included partnerships and individuals with ideas who could now get capital to put to work. "It was wonderful to watch," said Luther Hodges. He prophesied that some of these will be large corporations in the next twenty to thirty years.

To attract large industry, North Carolina had to revise its tax structure, Governor Hodges was advised. He asked the 1955 Legislature to authorize a study, and it was done. A commission was set up "to recommend changes in the basic tax system of the state and of the rates of taxation, together with the predicted revenue effects thereof, and the alternate sources of revenue, to the end that our revenue system may be stable and equitable, and yet so fair when compared with the tax structures of other states, that business enterprises and persons would be encouraged by the impact of the North Carolina Revenue Laws to move themselves and their business enterprises into the State of North Carolina."

The tax allocation formula was changed. Prior to that time North Carolina taxed the income of domestic and foreign corporations doing business in more than one state. The change was helpful to North Carolina corporations doing business in other states, as well as an attraction to industries in other states to locate in North Carolina.

The changes in formula placed North Carolina in a more competitive position among her sister states for new industry. It encouraged local corporations not to move home offices, sales offices, or accounting offices outside of the state as a means of reducing their income taxes. It demonstrated that we were willing to give not concessions but equal treatment to all businesses.

At a press conference following the tax changes, Governor Hodges announced a new $35 million expansion of R. J. Reynolds Tobacco Company—owing to the new allocation formula.

North Carolina Revenue Commissioner James Currie reported in November 1958:

> In general, corporations manufacturing in this state and selling on the national market have on the whole benefited from the change which eliminated discrimination against multi-state manufacturers. And, in general, corporations manufacturing elsewhere and selling in North Carolina experienced a tax increase. The net result has been to produce more equitable measure of the amount of income earned in North Carolina by multi-state companies regardless of place of charter.

It was a good beginning, and Governor Hodges had led the way, but he had to make it plain he was not Santa Claus bringing industry to all communities and allocating manufacturing plants and payrolls from a great big bag. He was making a speech in an eastern North Carolina town, and in the introduction the mayor said "I want to say to Governor Hodges that I want him to bring us industry."

"I will not bring you industry," Governor Hodges replied. "The governor cannot bring you industry. My goal is to get certain state taxes changed and certain attitudes in the state transformed. Then many communities in the state, such as this town, can organize and prepare for new industry. You must sell your communities to prospective industry. The state and its governor offer you leadership and guidance. But the **point of sale** for each industrial prospect is right here—in your own hands."

North Carolina's bread-and-butter problem was approached then from an entirely new angle. The state had two deep water ports, one at Morehead City, the other at Wilmington. Reorganizing and pumping new blood into the State Ports Authority, and launching a creative public relations program, Governor Hodges arranged for new designs that would be modern and up-to-date—both in facilities and services, and comparable with good ports in other states. The plan worked. From gross revenues at the two ports in 1955 of $471,000, there was a prompt increase in business. Revenues were $1,500,000 in 1959-60. The net profit increase was even more impressive—from $43,000 in 1954-55 to $482,000 in 1960-61. Tonnage figures were up and growing. More North Carolina products were moving through the ports in export trade and more imports from abroad were coming in through the terminals at Wilmington and Morehead City.

Hodges went after large industry much as big game hunters go after and bring back what they look for. He organized safaris, Tar Heels participating in these became known nation-wide as "industry hunters." Governor Hodges led expeditions to tell "The North Carolina Story." A trip to New York City was organized in 1957. In response to the governor's call for volunteers to go to New York as salesmen for North Carolina, seventy-five representatives of communities from all over the state joined the party. They paid their own way.

The Conservation and Development Department furnished lists of names of "prospects" in New York. The industry hunters, working in pairs, made calls on the prospects. The twosomes didn't promote their own communities, but the whole state of North Carolina. They told of North Carolina's business climate, of research and education, of equitable taxes, good health, and fine highways.

Newspaper editorial cartoonists pictured Luther Hodges on horseback, attired something like the hero of Morgan's Confederate Raiders of Civil War fame. He wore a plume in his hat, and a Stars and Bars flag bore the sign "Hodges' Raiders." On his drawn sword was the banner with the insignia "Y'All Come."

In his speeches at New York dinners and luncheons and breakfasts (attended by hundreds of New Yorkers) the North Carolina governor declared he was not trying to steal industry from other states. Instead, said Hodges:

> If you are thinking of expanding your manufacturing activities or of finding a new location in order to serve your markets better, especially in the Southeast, you should certainly consider North Carolina. There are no tax gimmicks or anything free offered. North Carolina is on the move and offers those things that a progressive corporation would like to have, namely an opportunity to live in a good community in a good state and make a profit.

Queen Elizabeth receives a gift from Gov. Luther Hodges, 1957. The Queen attended a football game between the University of North Carolina and the University of Maryland.

The Tar Heels appeared on TV shows and on radio programs, local and national, telling of North Carolina and its unique industry hunt. This bit of press agentry was arranged by "adopted" North Carolinians, known as Honorary Tar Heels—an organization of newspapermen and broadcasters who are invited frequently to North Carolina for outings. The Honorary Tar Heels made all the contacts and arrangements for broadcast and similar appearances.

When the industry hunters went on another safari in 1958—this time to Philadelphia—the number of volunteers grew to 122. It was in Philadelphia that Hodges stressed the novel venture in North Carolina: The Research Triangle. In central North Carolina are three major universities of national standing: The University of North Carolina in Chapel Hill, Duke University at Durham and North Carolina State University in Raleigh. These institutions have scientists and other personnel of high caliber, capable of lending to an envisioned great new research center manpower that would spur research enterprise useful to the nation—and, incidentally, promote industrial growth in North Carolina. The area became known as the Research Triangle Park of North Carolina.

Success of the industry-hunting expedition in several other big cities incited the Tar Heels to an even more ambitious plan: a trip to Europe! Sixty-eight North Carolinians flew in October 1959, to London and on to Western Europe. They visited business leaders and held luncheons and dinners in England, the Netherlands, Germany, Switzerland,

France and Belgium. "The British guests warmly received my luncheon speech," wrote Gov. Hodges. Several times they cried, 'hear, hear' and hand-thumped the table tops as I outlined what North Carolina was doing to raise its own standard of living and to offer the best possible economic opportunity to its people and to those who settle there."

In Zurich, Gov. Hodges reminded businessmen that a Swiss, Baron de Graffenried, had founded a North Carolina town and named it for Bern, in Switzerland. But before he founded New Bern, De Graffenried demanded that a certain number of gold pieces be paid to him. Gov. Hodges added to his audience, "From what I see and hear today in Zurich I don't think you Swiss have changed very much." The Swiss responded with laughter and applause.

Gov. Hodges, toting up results of the European trip, said 79 people showed a definite interest in the ports of Wilmington and Morehead City; 12 in the Research Triangle; 26 in possible manufacturing operations; 41 in sales outlets; seven in licensing agreements, and 83 in a general interest in North Carolina. The Department of Conservation and Development followed up on the trip with letters. The first European manufacturing plant to be located in North Carolina as a result of the trade and industry mission was announced just eight months later. Pleuger Submersible Pump Co. of Hamburg announced that its first U. S. plant would be in Statesville, N. C.

During the six full years of the Hodges administration, 1,053 new industries came to North Carolina.

Expansions were made by 1,405 of the industries already in the state. New industries represented a total capital investment of $509,016,000; jobs for 79,588; a payroll of $248,461,000. New and old industries combined (including expansions) reported capital investment for the period of $1,114,950,000; jobs for 140,233; and a payroll of $437,553,000.

It was a cooperative venture of North Carolinians under Luther Hodges' leadership. On one of the expeditions, a man who had volunteered sent his regrets at the last minute. He reluctantly backed out—on doctor's orders. The physician advised, "It's foolish for you, in your condition, to try to keep up with Luther Hodges. It's not good for your health."

Chapter Twelve

School and Race Solutions

The press, including the Raleigh correspondents, were grateful to Luther Hodges. He always made copy. He was so busy, and so willing to talk about North Carolina and its progress, that the day never passed that he did not have something new, different, and often astonishing to say. Reporters also found him disarmingly nonsecretive. When they asked a question, the reply was prompt, to the point, full, and in accord with his goals for the good of the state. He abided by the tenet: "I can answer quickly and honestly and confidently, because I don't have to remember what I told them the last time. Just tell the truth, and all will be well." His comments and retorts in press conferences were apparently without hesitation. This made for a friendly press, too; for the sincerity and ability of the man showed through. Newsmen knew there was nothing devious about Luther Hodges.

Hugh Haynie, the editorial cartoonist for the **Greensboro Daily News**, could kid the Governor, such as his illustration of Hodges in full medieval armor riding a steed and bearing a lance. The title was "Luther, the Lion-Hearted." The knight in shining armor impersonating the governor could be battling lobbyists who wanted to impose a sales tax on food, or he could be wrestling with other formidable interests trying to derive unjust benefits from the state. Governor Hodges reproduced many of the cartoons in his book, **Businessman in the Statehouse.**

The press often accompanied him on trips throughout the state, and Hodges was a traveling and speaking governor. In three hurricanes in the state in 1955, the governor flew to the coast and watched the devastation even as the winds were blowing. One photograph shows Gov. Hodges in rain hat amid the torrents of a 90-mile-an-hour gale. There was not much he could do to stop the hurricanes, but it made North Carolinians feel better to know he was on the job. Further, he was quick to bring financial and rehabilitation relief to those who were unhoused or otherwise harmed by the storms. It didn't hurt him politically. One Outer Banks fisherman, asked why they voted so heavily for Hodges in the 1956 campaign, said simply: "He rid out the hurricanes with us."

The **Addresses and Papers of Luther Hartwell Hodges** during those six years take up three thick volumes, edited by Prof. James W. Patton of the Southern Historical Collection in Chapel Hill. Besides his major legislative and message-to-the-people speeches, he hit the banquet and chamber of commerce and church circuits. He spoke on Veterans

Day, Safe Driving Day, Thanksgiving Day, National Guard Muster Day, and on many special occasions, such as the groundbreaking for the G. E. Plant at Hendersonville, N. C. He talked to farmers' meetings. He addressed the bankers at their annual convention. He was heard by thousands at the Roan Mountain Rhododendron Festival. He made speeches to judges, to college students and faculty, to newspapermen, to YMCA's, to art devotees, to garment workers, to parent-teacher associations, to the Women's National Democratic Club, to motor carriers, manufacturers, teachers, doctors, wholesalers, retailers, orphans, delinquent girls, traffic safety advocates, and scores of other groups.

When he spoke to the New York City Rotary Club June 21, 1956, it was something of a homecoming, for Luther had been president of the New York club in 1946. He returned to New York as Governor of North Carolina and the leader on an industry hunt. He said to his fellow Rotarians who had asked him to speak on the issue of school segregation in North Carolina:

> This talk today will not be an attempt to justify the North Carolina attitude regarding racial difficulties, although I would like to tell you just a little of the situation in our state. Out of approximately 1,000,000 school children, we have a Negro enrollment of some 300,000, and we employ as many Negro school teachers as do the seven states of New York, Pennsylvania, Illinois, Ohio, Michigan, California and Indiana all put together. The percentage of Negro residents in the various counties of our state varies from 0.3 percent in Mitchell County to

66.4 percent in Warren County and the percent of Negro children in Warren County is 72.9 percent. This means to us that we must deal with the segregation problem on a local community approach. . . .

Gov. Hodges addressed the New York City Rotary Club sometime after the United States Supreme Court ruled that segregation in the public schools should be ended and also a few months before he was to present a plan to the North Carolina General Assembly whereby North Carolina could comply with the court's decision and yet not upset too drastically the system of public education in North Carolina.

Southern states, where most of the Negroes of the nation lived, considered themselves hard hit by the High Court decision. Segregation, or separateness, was a way of life. It was apparent that deep-seated prejudices would create difficulties, for two primary reasons: (1) a sizeable number of people were prepared to say "Don't give an inch; defy the Supreme Court!"; (2) there were a few who said, "Let's desegregate immediately, post-haste," who wanted to go full speed on the process of integration —even though the Court itself had called only for "deliberate speed."

North Carolina did not follow either extreme. It watched with growing disenchantment the policy of massive resistance practiced by the State of Virginia which resulted in closing of schools in a number of places—no schools for Negro or white.

Governor Umstead had appointed a commission to look into what North Carolina ought to do, immediately after the Supreme Court had made its decision in May 1954, upsetting the principle of separate-but-equal, which had been the practice in the South for 60 years. In 1955 Gov. Hodges reconstituted the commission, again naming its chairman, Thomas J. Pearsall of Rocky Mount, to work out a plan for North Carolina.

The commission was composed of liberals and conservatives—the let's-go-slow people and the people who thought faster acceleration was necessary. Tom Pearsall exerted masterful leadership in working out a middle-of-the-road compromise that was workable. The "Pearsall Plan" was a means of obeying the law, yet buying time until people were more in a frame of mind to accept what many believed to be inevitable.

Governor Hodges spoke on a statewide broadcast TV-radio network. He pointed to a former decision by Federal Judge John J. Parker of the Fourth Circuit Court of Appeals who had said the Constitution "does not require integration. It merely forbids discrimination."

The Pearsall Committee planned what was called "safety valve" legislation—a plan to siphon off some of the steam of emotions that the race question and the Supreme Court decision had aroused, to do what was fair, and to save the schools.

At the same time the Pearsall Plan was not a case of foot-dragging. "It was not conceived as a delaying action," said Hodges. "It was the best thing we could figure out, and it tried to meet the situation and the temper of the people and at the same time did preserve the schools. I would not change the decision we made at that time."

After weeks of study, debate, compromise, accepting and rejecting, the Pearsall recommendations prepared for consideration at a special session of the General Assembly were submitted with these specifics: tuition grants could be given by the state so that children of either race who were assigned against their wishes to mixed schools could have their way paid at private schools; any local community faced with what it considered to be an intolerable situation could close the schools in that community, by popular vote.

Gov. Hodges explained the several bills and the purposes behind them. "Immediate closing of a school by accumulative action on account of integration would obviously deprive the people of any say so in the matter," he said. "On the other hand, immediate integration would create untold difficulties and would also deprive the people of North Carolina of a choice in the matter."

To those who said nothing at all should be done (allowing the tide of events to take North Carolina into the unknown in the segregation-integration issue) Gov. Hodges said, "The end result of this course of action or inaction could easily have been integration with no choice and no relief, with the consequence of our schools being starved to death for lack of legislative and public support."

The Pearsall Plan was explained in meetings held in several parts of the state. Gov. Hodges' chief aide Paul Johnston remembers a meeting in one little town where the thinking behind and the provisions of the plan were explained. After the meeting a farmer came to Paul Johnston and said, in the manner of one explaining a complex matter to a child, "Mr. Johnston, don't you know that the people of this town are not going to vote to **close** the schools?"

Johnston smiled and said, "They might not, at that."

The Pearsall Committee had faith that North Carolinians would not deliberately close their local schools—if there were safety valve arrangements, such as the tuition grants, and if the leaders of the state and communities were permitted elbow room to permit moderation.

When, several years later, the Pearsall Plan was termed unconstitutional by the Supreme Court, certain liberal leaders of the State who had counseled integration from the beginning were quick to say, "I told you so." But Luther Hodges, Tom Pearsall and others had bought time. Integration was taking place without upheaval. The schools were not abandoned. There was no "massive resistance" in North Carolina.

Paul Johnston also calls the "highly sophisticated" Pearsall Plan and its expert handling "the major accomplishment of the Hodges Administration." There are those who say that bringing in new industry and educational attainments were his big contribution. But Johnston believes that the master-

ful way Gov. Hodges steered the course in what
came to be known as the Pupil Assignment Act and
other measures transcended his other eminently
praiseworthy achievements. "He allowed the state
to be a state of dignity and intelligence in the eyes
of the nation," said Johnston. The U. S. State Department's "Voice of America" honored North Carolina
by asking Gov. Hodges to broadcast to the world how
North Carolina had handled its school integration
problem. Hodges complied.

Paul Johnston believed Luther Hodges to be one
of America's greatest administrators. "He could lead
and direct any large industry in the country today.
He has great executive ability. He is able to select
and choose what work to undertake and when to do
it. He seems to know which plans will work and
which won't. He is able to move a mass of people. He
can call upon creative minds and then take out what
ideas he can use. Many people with creative minds
can throw out a lot of ideas, many of them unwork-
able. Luther Hodges is able to extract the ones that
can be applied. When he works with men, there is a
melding of ideas. He does this with the work of
many people. He knows how to use their talents. It
is not easy to delegate authority, not simple to know
how to use a staff. But Gov. Hodges can do it, and
he can follow up that delegation of authority to
evaluate performance."

In managing his staff in the Capitol Gov. Hodges
asked for reports on actions taken as well as actions
about to be taken. His reins were not loose, nor were
they tight—at least not so tight that they interfered

with performance. "Yet he finds out who is performing and who isn't," said Johnston.

Governor Hodges keeps a clean desk. "He's tidy to a fault," said Johnston, "and busy all the time. There's no chit-chat during office hours."

Johnston's assessment conforms with the views of others who have worked with Luther Hodges. Johnston can also testify to the times when the governor does let down and relax. "It's true he can take it easy when he fishes," he said. "I went out in a rowboat with him once near Mobile, Alabama. We sat there in the rowboat for about an hour. He hardly moved a muscle. He seemed calm and free, even though he didn't catch a single fish that day." Paul Johnston, on the other hand, could hardly keep still. "I was squirming," he said. "I wanted to get the hell out of there."

In further philosophy about the practical idealism of the governor, Paul Johnston has another appraisal —that Luther Hartwell Hodges is sincerely dedicated to the public good. Queries were put to Johnston: "Is Gov. Hodges really that devoted to mankind, to the public interest, to the general welfare? Can any man be that good? Is there no bit of sham in his makeup?"

"Hodges really means it and there is no fooling," said Johnston. "He has the same sincerity that Franklin D. Roosevelt had and that Lyndon B. Johnson has. He has that regard for the masses. He's a true liberal, and he's pragmatic."

On several occasions in Raleigh, the governor was approached by people who sought special favors.

They had contributed something—perhaps to the Hodges campaign for reelection in 1956—and were calling to ask for something in return. "At such times Gov. Hodges seemed to be puzzled," said Paul Johnston. "He would tell the visitors when he had to turn them down, 'But I thought you were doing that for the state; I didn't think you were doing it for me personally.' " Hodges knew what the favor-seekers were driving at. But his air of innocence disarmed them completely.

In short, Luther Hodges is, according to Paul Johnston, "not a provincial man; he is a citizen of the United States. He brought a breadth of experience and cosmopolitan thinking into the affairs of the state in North Carolina. He was head of one of the nation's great industries; he was a top echelon figure in business. He had lived in New York seven years and was President of the New York City Rotary Club. He had been in international service for his nation, and he was courageously dedicated to the good of his home state."

"The press thinks it needs more space," said Ed Rankin, the governor's secretary. He told Gov. Hodges that the press had complained, politely, that it was cramped, didn't have enough room in putting out their stories about the work of the 1959 General Assembly.

"What do you suggest?" said Gov. Hodges.

"I believe a temporary structure could be built," said Rankin. "There's room at the East Portico of the Capitol."

"I though the suggestion had merit," wrote Hodges in **Businessman in the Statehouse.** Engineers and architects checked it out, and they designed a neat, prefabricated temporary structure that could be placed in the Portico floor space—and removed after the Legislature adjourned. The Council of State approved the project.

But the project was criticized. The Raleigh News and Observer said it was a "desecration." The Dean of the N. C. State College School of Design, Henry L. Kamphoefner, was quoted: "an architectural affront." The Secretary of State said it would look like "the nose on a buffalo."

Governor Hodges avoided argument. He founded a new organization, the "Order of Buffalo." Certificates were printed, on which a buffalo was sketched. It read, in part:

To all to whom these presents shall come— greeting:

This is to certify that the Order of the Buffalo has been organized for the solemn and special purpose of supervising closely and carefully the installation of a temporary and detachable nose on our Ancient Buffalo. This is to certify further that we share a common affection for the Buffalo and will unite our efforts to guarantee the complete removal of said nose from our Buffalo immediately after it has served its express purposes.

At the bottom of the certificate were the names of Thad Eure, "founder and president;" Henry Bridges, "secretary and auditor;" **News and Observer** Editor Jonathan Daniels; and Dean Kamphoefner. Luther Hodges' name was signed as "keep-er of the nose." The certificates made a big hit with the press corps. They named their new home, "The Buffalo's Nose."

Luther Hodges met criticism with humor, solved a problem of space, pleased even his critics, and added luster to his already high standing with the press.

Chapter Thirteen

The Research Triangle

Hugh Morton was driving. Governor Luther Hodges was in the front seat beside him. Ahead was a roadside fruit stand. "Let's stop there," said Luther. He liked fresh fruit and made a practice of stopping at markets. In visiting cities in foreign countries he invariably would take time out to go to flower markets, vegetable stands and other outdoor food displays. It was 1956 and Hodges was running for his first full term as governor. Hugh Morton was one of his publicity men. They bought apples and drove on. When Morton had eaten his apple down to the core, he lowered the window half way and tossed the core out.

"Governor Hodges exploded," reports Morton. "He began to berate me for throwing the apple core out on the highway. I was so rattled I damned near wrecked the car. He saw I was having trouble with the wheel so he subsided quickly."

Then in more calm fashion, the governor lectured Morton on how motorists should avoid littering the highways. Morton pleaded guilty, since he had been caught red-handed, but he defended himself mildly, pleading extenuating circumstances. At least, he said, throwing out an apple core, a perishable thing, was not the same as throwing out a bag or a paper cup or a beer can. "We finally compromised," said Morton, "and concluded that perhaps a rabbit or a bird had eaten the apple core and that the highway was not unsightly because of the happenstance." But Morton had an opportunity to witness the governor's spontaneous and justifiable outburst. "He did raise his voice at me," said Morton. "It was the maddest he has ever been at me, and he jumped on me with both feet."

Hugh Morton is an independent businessman, photographer and promoter, and has a celebrated flair for public relations. He made a color motion picture of Luther Hodges' life during the 1956 campaign, and it was shown on television stations and at political gatherings. Morton owns Grandfather Mountain, a western North Carolina tourist resort attraction, and he is responsible more than anyone else for bringing the superannuated battleship **USS North Carolina** to a final resting place at a Wilmington harbor where tourists flock to it in tens of thousands every year.

Although the opposition in the Democratic Party was not formidable, Luther didn't take any chances. He conducted a spirited campaign, as though he were "running scared." Harold Makepeace of Sanford was campaign manager. Makepeace had helped him in his campaign for lieutenant governor. In the campaign headquarters principals were Paul Johnston, Ed Rankin and Bob Giles of his staff; Hugh Morton; and two newspapermen, Al Resch of Siler City and Mutt Burton of Reidsville. Ben Trotter of Leaksville also devoted his time and skills.

They raised $30,000, and when the election was over and Hodges had won, it was found that the campaign had cost only $22,500. Gov. Hodges had his manager go over the list of campaign contributors and returned to each contributor 25 percent of what he had given. The $7,500 left over and returned was the subject of national news attention. Few people had ever heard anything like it before.

When the Legislature met in 1957, Gov. Hodges presented North Carolina's first billion dollar budget. The Governor's State of the State message to the Legislature could have been entitled "The North Carolina Dream." He said:

> I see a land of thriving industry of many kinds—manufacturing, agricultural, research; with plants distributed throughout the state— east, west, north and south, set well apart on our countryside and in well-planned small towns and medium-sized cities, drawing their workers from all the surrounding areas, without the slum conditions, the polluted air, the unmanageable congestion, and the other unwanted characteristics of the present typical American industrial center. This is a land where all workers are land owners and home owners, rather than modern-day cliff dwellers cramped in gloomy rented flats and furnished rooms; a land with prospering farms producing many different crops and no longer dependent for their existence on a one-

or-two-crop market. I see in every community well-constructed, modernly equipped and modernly run schools, staffed by adequately trained and adequately paid teachers, supported by an enthusiastic people who demand nothing less than the best for all children. This is a land where all citizens have sufficient economic opportunity, spare time and education to enjoy the best there is in life through private pursuits supplemented by public cultural and recreational facilities. And in this land, looking out over all else, there are towers of colleges and universities—for it is an enlightened land—and the spires of many churches—for it is a moral land.

This is the vision, the North Carolina dream. And it is not an unattainable thing. We have the great heritage, with past leaders who have shown us what courage and faith and hard work can do. We have the people, and the natural resources to turn this dream into eventual reality, if we but work and continue to have courage and faith in our own abilities. You and I, in the all too few years remaining to any of us, can do no more than to lead our state a little of the way, but if we do this, and hand over to those who come after us the courage and faith which were handed to us, then, God willing, this vision of North Carolina will become her destiny.

The world since 1950 has experienced a national and international research boom. During and since World War II and since the beginning of the space race, there have been scientific thrusts leading to peaceful uses of atomic energy, automation, medical advances and investigations into human behavior. University scientists are assigned important roles in the development. In certain university centers, or clusters of educational institutions, there have developed certain research centers—conspicuously in New England, in the Boston-Cambridge sector, in California, and in the Chicago midwest. Utilizing the presence of brains and talent on the campuses and supplementing these with growing organizations of specialist personnel, the regional research centers have undertaken a sizeable proportion of the tasks—assigned from the federal government, from private foundations, from volunteer health agencies, from business and industry. Accompanying these research park developments is another growth: new industry and private and public research centers attracted to the same spot, and drawn by the magnetism of the others.

The idea had been discussed before, by sociologist Howard W. Odum of Chapel Hill. In 1952 he proposed a research center utilizing the talent available at the University in Chapel Hill and at N. C. State College in Raleigh. Making it a "triangle" idea and bringing in Duke University was the suggestion of a Greensboro construction man, Romeo Guest. He prepared a brochure. The three universities were pictured in a triangle, the points of the triangle, Durham, Chapel Hill and Raleigh. The combined potentiality for research was stressed. Guest also envisioned research laboratories inside the triangle, and new industry radiating throughout the state.

When the idea was broached to Gov. Hodges, he immediately and favorably reacted. He discussed it with other people. He looked on the Research Triangle as a method of promoting the state and attracting industry. "The key to its development was cooperation among the University of North Carolina, Duke University, State College, my office and the business and industrial leadership of the state," wrote Hodges. "There was a need for organization, and, with North Carolina's future at stake, there was also a need for the maximum amount of action."

Hodges appointed a Governor's Research Triangle Committee. He asked Robert M. Hanes of Winston-Salem—the man who had asked Hodges to help him in ECA in West Germany in 1951—to become chairman. "He accepted," said Gov. Hodges, "and spent much time, money and effort to make this dream a reality." A working committee composed of chief officers and science specialists at the three institutions began planning. In 1956 a full-time staff member was hired, George L. Simpson Jr., professor and associate of the late Howard W. Odum. In 1957 Dr. Simpson proposed: (1) that efforts be made to make industry and government agencies acquainted with the research sources and environment of the Research Triangle; (2) that a research park be established in the center of the Triangle; (3) that a research institute be established to do contract research for industry and government. Simpson's plan was adopted. Information was sent to a thousand companies across the United States. Emphasis was put on the area's resources in a number of fields, including pharmaceutical, electronic and chemical. Chairman Hanes furnished the funds for travel and other expenses. The response was gratifying; several companies expressed interest in the Triangle area.

They indicated they might consider settling laboratories there.

A first need was to buy the land. To purchase the
land, money was needed, a lot of it. To get the
money an "angel" was a necessity. To approach the
angel, a salesman was required. Luther Hodges was
the salesman. Conservation and Development Director Bill Saunders suggested to Gov. Hodges the
name of Karl Robbins of New York. Robbins had
owned textile mills in North Carolina and was interested in the state. Both Saunders and Hodges
knew him well. Governor Hodges invited Robbins
to breakfast at the Mansion. Others present were
Saunders and Prof. George Simpson. The four
talked about the Triangle scheme. Gov. Hodges had
been speaking about five minutes when Robbins
interrupted him, "You need not say anything more,
Luther. I understand. It is a wonderful idea and a
money-maker. I'll back you and will put a million
dollars in the project." Robbins got Romeo Guest to
handle park matters, and buying of 5,000 acres of
land began soon after. The Research Triangle Park
was on the move. It was near a busy airport, had
frontage on two railroads, and was criss-crossed with
four major highways.

Archie K. Davis, Wachovia Bank and Trust
Company's board chairman, was persuaded to take
over the job of raising money for the Research
Institute and the Park's development. Davis came
up with a new idea: to discard the idea of a profit-
making land project and instead make it a nonprofit
agency benefiting North Carolina as a whole, and

the three universities in particular. To do that it would be necessary to buy out Karl Robbins' interest in the Research Triangle Park, which amounted in 1958 to several hundreds of thousands in land purchases. "Archie was optimistic, and I was hopeful," said Gov. Hodges. On January 9, 1959, Hanes and Hodges announced $1,425,000 had been contributed by business and industry in North Carolina for the further development of the state's Research Triangle as a center of industrial and governmental research. One of the first uses made of the money was to make a grant of $500,000 to get the Research Triangle Institute going.

A director of the Research Triangle Institute was hired, George R. Herbert, who was former executive associate director of the Stanford Research Institute in California.

The Research Triangle Institute was designed to support itself ultimately through contract research for industry and government, using its own professional staff in its own laboratory buildings. Revenues received paid operating costs, bought buildings and equipment needed for research investigations and provided capital for growth. A Research Triangle Foundation was formed, and it was made plain that the institute was "owned" by the three Universities. George Herbert assembled a small staff and began to look for national research contracts. The first contract (for $160,900) came in June, 1959, from the Atomic Energy Commission, for research in its development of isotopes. By the end of the summer

Herbert reported $400,000 in contracts and 26 employed staff members.

During the same summer Chemstrand Corporation (now Monsanto) announced it would build a multi-million dollar chemical fiber research laboratory in the Research Triangle Park. Later in 1959, Gov. Hodges announced that the Dreyfus Foundation of New York had given $2.5 million to the Research Triangle Institute to set up a national center for study of polymer or synthetic fiber chemistry. Then other laboratories came in: The U. S. Forest Service, Regional Laboratory, International Business Machines; the national Environmental Health Sciences Center; Technitrol, Inc., producer of computer components; American Association of Textile Chemists and Colorists; the N. C. Science and Technology Research Center; Beaunit Fibers; National Air Pollution Center; the Regional Education Laboratory for the Carolinas and Virginia; the Triangle Universities Computation Center; and the Data Processing Laboratory of the National Center for Health Statistics.

In 1966 the Institute owned six buildings representing an investment of $3,179,376. The staff had grown to 282, and the payroll for the year was $2,696,122. Total revenues for 1966 were $4,174,463.

Gov. Luther Hodges summed it up:

The Research Triangle is an idea that has produced a reality—the idea that the scientific brains and research talents of three institutions, and their life of research in many fields, could provide the background and stimulation of research for the benefit of the state and nation. In a way, the Research Triangle is the marriage of North Carolina's ideals for higher education and its hopes for material progress."

To assertions that Luther Hodges should be called the "businessman governor," others sometimes reply, "but he should be called the 'education governor,' too." For Hodges' efforts were turned toward harmonizing the mutual forces of business and education. The Research Triangle Institute is a prime example. In his book, **Businessman in the Statehouse,** is a chapter, "Education—First on the Budget." His first sentence is "Education is the chief business of the state of North Carolina." That meant the public school system and the publicly-supported colleges and universities. Gov. Hodges succeeded in founding industrial and vocational training centers in the state. Over 20,000 people were enrolled by 1960, training men and women in modern techniques of new industry, and others for work in industry long established in North Carolina. Under Governor Hodges the state established a Board of Higher Education to exercise certain guidance and growth for the 4-year colleges in the state, the two-year junior colleges and the consolidated University of North Carolina system which was made up of the University in Chapel Hill, the University at Greensboro and the North Carolina State University in Raleigh. It was during Governor Hodges' administration that William Friday was named President of the consolidated University, and the University under his leadership has made advances unmatched in the history of the state.

William Friday, who was secretary of the Consolidated University of North Carolina when Gordon Gray was president, was called to Governor Hodges' office in Raleigh on January 4, 1956. "The trustees' executive committee and the governor were there," said Friday. "Governor Hodges told me that the trustees wanted to ask me to become acting president of the University." Later the trustees were pleased with the way Friday was handling the job and the "acting" was subtracted from his title. "I worked with Governor Hodges from that time to the end of his administration," said Friday. "We had contacts on many matters affecting the University, its budget and appropriations and its activities, and in developing the Research Triangle, University administration and legislative actions—together with some of the plans he was evolving for the state. He had a way of bringing in talent that he thought would be useful, and he counted on the abilities of people in the three institutions of the University."

President Friday declared that Gov. Hodges gave him full support and knew "the difference between policy, belonging to trustees, and operations, devolving to the administration." The governor "helped us when we needed help, and never interfered in administration," said President Friday. Gov. Hodges aided the University of North Carolina in securing "substantial increases" in faculty salaries and other essential support. "Gov. Hodges is an aggressive, dynamic individual," said Friday, "who kept a place of primacy for the university in his thinking and acton when he was governor. The University profited from his leadership."

Of his Alma Mater, Gov. Hodges wrote in his book:

I would like to testify that wherever I have been in this country I heard nothing but praise for the University of North Carolina and for the quality of work that it has done and is doing. If we by carelessness or by failure, do not support both in money and in influence the consolidated University, we can hurt the state as a whole. I have been asked a score of times by people from other states and by correspondents and public officials, "What is the secret of North Carolina and its progress as compared to its sister states in the South? Why does it seem to be so liberal or so moderate? Why doesn't it do as the other states have done?" These were hard questions to answer, but I have said generally that it is because of our educational system as a whole—good teachers' colleges, both white and Negro. But basically it is because in the old days before other colleges were built up to serve the regions within the state, the University of North Carolina established in its graduates a desire for public service in the community and in the nation. It tried to be of service to the state in intellectual leadership; it tried to challenge its graduates, its alumni, and the citizens generally to see the state's needs as a whole, to look at all sides of a question.

Beyond the colleges and universities and the vocational schools, Gov. Hodges also saw another need, to cope with increasing enrollments and to simplify the transition from high schools to higher education or a career based on the special education afforded by the community colleges. The 1957 General Assembly authorized community colleges in

Governor Luther Hodges standing in front of the North Carolina State Capitol Building in Raleigh, 1956. The white carnation in his lapel was a trademark.

strategic locations in the state, where students could commute from home to classes. The community colleges are a combination of post-high school, junior college and vocational-technical schools. The cost was borne three ways: by the state, by the local communities, and by the students themselves.

Luther Hodges is known as the man "who pushed politics off the highways of North Carolina." He found that the State Highway Commission was acting almost autonomously in the state and handling tremendous amounts of money, some of it apparently used for political purposes. The Highway Commission was also closely tied with the State Prisons System.

The governor brought the Highway Commission closer under state supervision, eliminated some of the doubtful ways of financial operations. He also set up the prisons system apart from the Highway Commission, to the lasting benefit of both.

In the rejuvenated Prisons System, an enlightened new penology policy was put into practice—the work-release privilege to certain classes of prisoners when recommended by the sentencing judge. The plan allowed a prisoner to work on a regular job outside the prison. He spent each night behind bars, but worked for outside business or industry during the day—and was paid for it. It was an excellent training program and a rehabilitation innovation that made a prisoner better prepared to return to society after his final release. Gov. Hodges treasures a letter from a prisoner who wrote to his supervisor:

This is a word of thanks to you and your assistants for the recent consideration given me. I am now on work release, and I cannot express in words my appreciation to you . . . and the Parole Board. As I cannot express my appreciation in words, I shall express it in my work. The faith and consideration you have placed in me shall not be in vain.

I shall do my best to make parole so that I can go to college. I have determined in my heart to pay my debt to my state and clear my name by asking God for his forgiveness.

Luther H. Hodges Jr., son of Governor Hodges.

Chapter Fourteen

Nine U. S. Governors in Russia

Governors of nine American states visited Russia in 1959. The Institute of International Education, an organization that sponsors student exchanges, arranged the journey. Expenses were paid by the Alfred P. Sloan Foundation and the Rockefeller Brothers Fund. Governor Luther Hodges, one of the nine, was guardedly optimistic about what might be achieved on the tour. "If we can get enough exchange of visits to bread down some of the suspicion, we may ultimately get a better understanding," he wrote in a trip report from Orly Airport in Paris, on his way to Moscow. No state or federal funds were involved—only the private funds, in the hope of fostering improved relations between east and west.

Before leaving the United States the governors assembled in Washington and were briefed by Secretary of State Christian Herter. They also talked with President Eisenhower. President Eisenhower asked them to stop again in Washington on their return trip to tell him about their experiences. Governor Leroy Collins of Florida was spokesman for the party, and the others were Robert Meyner of New Jersey, Cecil Underwood of West Virginia, William Stratton of Illinois, George Davis of North Dakota, Robert Smylie of Idaho, Steve McNichols of Colorado, George Clyde of Utah. Noting the ages of the members, Gov. Hodges said, "Although I thought I felt as young as any governor in the group, I found that I was the oldest governor in the party!" He was 61.

A Paris newspaperman asked Hodges what he expected to do in the USSR. "To learn all we can from our visit, by being interested, by being friendly, and yet being realistic." He told the newsman of a talk they had heard before leaving Washington by Soviet Ambassador Menshikov who had asked the governors to go to see his country "with an open mind." He said he thought Menshikov's counsel was "disarming" and he thought it was proper to say the governors were going, not as Democrats or Republicans, but as Americans on a friendly basis."

Flying into Russia the governors were wary of the indefiniteness of their schedule and the slight psychological pressure upon them because they didn't know what they could expect when they arrived in Moscow. The USSR had declined to give a complete itinerary; they had said, "Come on to Moscow. We will work it out after that." In his letter, Gov. Hodges wrote, "The Russians, as usual, leave things uncertain and keep everything uncertain in all its American relations, even a thing as simple as what's going to happen to this party of governors."

At the airport in Moscow they were met by a deputy of the Soviet Minister of Cultural Affairs, The deputy and his aides made speeches and shook hands with the governors; interpreters were helpful, and then all proceeded in automobiles twenty miles into Moscow, past Red Square and on to a hotel for tourists named the Sovietska. The accommodations were comfortable and pleasing.

The governors at the first meeting with Minister Zhukov, head of Cultural Affairs, asked for a complete schedule of events so that they would know where they were going and when. "Although we knew they had worked out a program for us for our present three-day stay here in Moscow they would not release it to us, and they only gave one engagement at a time." This must have been obnoxious to a man who plans ahead like Luther Hodges. But he only wrote, "This was tantalizing to some people but it worked out all right." The governors then met Chronotop-Vasily, the Chairman of the Presidium. With him were thirty deputies who control departments such as public works, education, health, agriculture. Gov. Hodges found Vasily "most attractive, affable and friendly." The governors were told of the organization of the U.S.S.R., especially the relationship of the state or regional group. He explained the 15 Republic States, each having a governor or chairman. They also were reminded of the Russian policy of state ownership of practically everything and control over jobs and ways of life under Communism. This included free medical care and hospitalization on doctors' orders, control over natural resources, and distribution of food and other necessities.

Responding, Governor Collins praised the Soviet Union for their achievements in scientific education and subsequent attainments, notably the first artificial satellite flight, Sputnik. The Russians were delighted. "You could see universal beaming on the part of the faces of all the people I was facing," Hodges wrote.

Of the Soviet Education Minister Aganasenko, the governor said, "I don't know when I have met a keener person. He is smart, almost arrogant, but he knew his stuff. He was completely sold on the Soviet system of education and compared it, gleefully, with the American system. He exaggerated and falsified somewhat about the American system, but he had enough truth to know in general what he was saying and to make his story a telling one."

Gov. Hodges, after touring with the other eight governors 12 to 15 hours a day without an afternoon's rest, decided he'd take a break and go off by himself. "I took a guide called Ibratt with a driver, and we went to the vegetable, fruit and flower markets," he said. The markets were crowded, prices high and quality "only fair." He stopped at a large department store, GUM, and watched the crowds and the sales. He visited the Kremlin. "Most of us think of the Kremlin as being grim, foreboding and full of vicious plans, but inside the Kremlin are beautiful churches and museums," he wrote.

The governors went to an Industrial and Agricultural Exposition, showing Soviet production, and followed it by watching a soccer game between Russians and Bulgarians. Enthusiasm was as high as at a Carolina-Duke football game, and the attendance was even more impressive—102,000 people.

In a conference with Minister of Economy Semenov at Leningrad, the governors inquired into industrial production and how needs are determined regionally. Gov. Hodges asked how they would go about organizing another textile mill if they found they needed another shirt factory, for instance. Semenov said it would be decided centrally whether it was needed, and if it were, they would work up a budget, appoint a manager, get the workers, and begin manufacture.

Gov. Hodges then said, "I have seen, or heard of, some hospital equipment that you have produced. It seems to me to be only a fraction of what it would cost in other countries. Certainly it's cheaper than we can make it in the United States. I wonder if you, Mr. Semenov, would consider building a plant like that in North Carolina? We are always looking for new industry in our state." Governor Hodges added that his question was one of policy as well as economics. Nevertheless, he wanted to get an answer.

"My question created amusement among all the Russians as well as our own party of governors," he wrote. Gov. Hodges said in his trip letter that he was only half-serious, but was eager to get Semenov's reaction. The Russian said he'd have to think it over, and that whatever the receptiveness to the idea it would be necessary for Governor Hodges to come through channels and present the matter formally. The next night Semenov approached Gov. Hodges and said his proposal had been discussed and that such a relationship "would be quite excellent."

Next day the governors visited a farm (where the manager, said Hodges, "looked like a character between Santa Claus and Theodore Roosevelt") that furnished milk and butter, eggs and chickens to the Leningrad market. At a dinner, "one of the grandest affairs I ever saw," there were twenty toasts, the whole event lasting three and a half hours. Repeatedly, Gov. Hodges had asked to see a tobacco factory, and finally he was shown through one. He carried North Carolina-made cigarettes wherever he went and passed them around.

At Tbellissi, the capital of the Georgian Republic, the governors were entertained and given treatment similar to that accorded in other places, except for one instance. The Minister of Agriculture for the Republic of Georgia gave a toast. He spoke for peaceful uses of the atom. His words left the direct impression that **only** Russia was interested in peace and peaceful uses. "This statement bothered me," wrote Hodges in his trip letter. He told Gov. Collins he'd like to take issue with what had been said.

Gov. Hodges told the Russians something of his impressions on the trip. These were favorable, he said. "I have met some of your people and have talked with them," he explained. "We call these people in American 'the man on the street.' It seems to me these people are as interested in peace as we are—and I can assure you that we are interested in maintaining peace in the world. But it seems to me from what I have heard here tonight, you do not understand that we, too, are dedicated to peace. You seem to think you are the only ones concerned with peace. You do not communicate to your people our desire for peace." Hodges then told of work in atomic research at N. C. State University, the peaceful use of the atom in raising peanuts. "You have no monopoly on peace," said Hodges, "We in America want it, and we pray for it." Gov. Hodges' message seemed to be well received and one of the Russians referred to it later in one of the many toasts.

The nine American governors met with Premier Nikita Khrushchev for nearly four hours and they talked over a gamut of topics. Gov. Hodges described Khrushchev as "cordial, almost effusive, dominating." The Premier said, "We are glad to see you folks from America, a country that is rich and strong. We want to be like you."

Gov. Hodges related:

He is a man of many moods. He is as smart a man as I have ever met—anywhere. He could be suave, ruthless, full of humor or show a clenched fist. He has a remarkable memory. He not only gave his side of the story with details and dates, but took on each of the seven governors who appeared uncertain on any point or who failed to know exactly what he was talking about. He out-maneuvered each person who really argued with him.

North Carolina's governor said to Khrushchev, "The exchange visits between your country and ours seem very helpful. We have found on our visit that your people appear friendly to Americans as individuals."

Khrushchev nodded as the interpreter translated Gov. Hodges' words. Then the governor said, "Mr. Khrushchev, you are a person of decision and action, and I want to make you a proposition that you spend at least $10 million additional next year in sending your people, particularly students, over to our country on an exchange basis, and we will see if we can persuade President Eisenhower to do the same thing."

Khrushchev smiled and replied, "I couldn't agree with you more, but where do we get the money? Where do we get the dollars? We can't forget the dollars, so how are we going to pay for it?"

Hodges countered, "You can reduce your spending for bombs and other things and use that money."

Khrushchev dismissed the idea immediately and changed the subject, going on a tirade about trade. He charged that the U.S.S.R. was being discriminated against.

Suddenly Khrushchev cooled off. He said calmly, "Shall we speak frankly on all matters, or shall we hedge and try to be nice to each other?"

"Speak as frankly as you will," said the governors, almost in one voice.

Khrushchev said:

What is it that you want? I think I can tell you what you want, or at least what we think you want, and you will never achieve it . . . You want to turn our people away from the Communist way of life they have adopted. You may try to do it, but you will never do it. We have made tremendous progress. Our satellite has been going for two years, and our cosmic rocket is now going around the sun . . . I know your great country. I know its history from the time it was founded, your breaking away from Colonial England and the marvelous progress you have made since that time which we want to emulate. But have you grown fat and smug, and are you looking down your noses at other people in the world? Have you forgotten to think realistically? Pardon me if I am rude.

At the conclusion of the interview, when Gov. Collins asked what message they could take back to President Eisenhower, the Russian leader folded his hands and replied in a low voice:

We want peace and friendship. We want peace with all nations, especially the United States of America, the biggest and the strongest . . . Let us work together . . .

It was in Samarkand, the old capital of Uzbekistan, that Luther Hodges blew his top. At another dinner when they were going through the routine of toasts, the Russian guide for the governors said with a sneer, "You seem to want to see old things more than you want to see the new and wonderful progress we are making. Governor Collins even asked me about camels. Everyone knows that camels were old-fashioned."

The governors took this without reply, and the guide continued his "toast."

"You want to see the churches. I can say to you that churches are absolutely no good. Churches mean nothing to our people. The only sensible answer is atheism!"

He concluded his toast to peace and friendship among nations. Obtaining Gov. Collins' permission to speak, Luther Hodges asked for the floor. He said:

> We appreciate the hospitality of our hosts and we are happy to share in the toast for peace and friendship between nations, but I thought that since we were in Samarkand as tourists and friends that some respect would be shown for our own feelings and beliefs. We have listened patiently and politely to all your propaganda about Soviet progress, but we don't have to listen to your propaganda about atheism. These Americans you are entertaining believe in God and in their own religious faiths — whether Christian or Jewish. I am weary of hearing you berate the church and God.

Gov. Hodges said in his trip report there was a "deadly silence for a whole minute." There was quick adjournment, and they returned to their hotel. His fellow governors expressed approval of what Gov. Hodges had said, and later even one of the Russians who was connected with the security department of government privately commended Gov. Hodges for his actions and said the local guide was out of order.

At one of the final meetings with the Russians, a governor asked the Soviet deputy leader, Anastas Mikoyan, what would the U.S.S.R. like to trade with the United States. "Can you tell us five things you want to sell and five things you want to buy?" Mikoyan was asked. Mikoyan replied that Russia would like to sell to the U.S.: (1) manganese ore— and lots of it, (2) chrome ore, (3) platinum, (4) cellulose, and (5) crabmeat.

He said Soviets want to buy: (1) entire textile plants, (2) plastic plants or products, (3) consumer goods, including tobacco, (4) pipes for gas lines, and (5) artificial leather goods.

In a message accompanying an account of his Russian trip, Gov. Hodges reflected:

> Our nations and our leaders must get along together, and I believe I can see signs of progress, even though the Soviet people have been misinformed by their government as to the United States and our desire for peace . . . I am no authority on either the Soviet Union or the Soviet system. I do not believe in the communist approach to life, but I am sure my experiences will cause me to be a better American citizen and a better citizen of the world."

Here is a fish Secretary of Commerce Luther Hodges caught 100 feet through the ice at McMurdo Sound near the South Pole. He suspended a line through a hole bored in the ice.

Chapter Fifteen

Life in the Mansion

On his way back home from Russia, Luther took the Polar route and stopped in Copenhagen to see Ensign Luther H. Hodges Jr. of the U. S. Navy. Earlier in 1959 Gov. Hodges had gone to Europe with his daughter, Betsy Bernard, and they had visited Luther Jr. and his wife at Villefranche, France, where Ensign Hodges was stationed with the 6th U. S. Fleet, abroad the **U.S.S. Des Moines.** It was one of the occasions the scattered Hodges family could get together, and they made the most of it. Governor Hodges then stopped in England and picked up Nancy Finlay's children who were in school. He took them back to the United States and on to North Carolina. They were joined there by Betsy Bernard's children. Martha and Luther Hodges took their grandchildren to the North Carolina mountain region near Brevard, specifically to a camp where the Hodges' daughters had gone. Betsy Bernard said, "He makes a hit with his grandchildren. They feel about him as I do. Everyone should have a father and a grandfather just like him.

Luther Hodges Jr. had graduated at Chapel Hill in 1957, tapped into the Order of Golden Fleece, just as his father had been, and was a member of Phi Beta Kappa. He was a member of the Navy ROTC at the University and won his commission. After his two year tour of military duty, he entered the Harvard Business School and worked in a bank during the summer. Then it was back to Chapel Hill, armed with a master's degree from Harvard. He worked with Prof. Joe Floyd of the Business School at Chapel Hill on a study, "Financing Industrial Growth." He also worked with Prof. Avery Cohan in research relating to uses of revenue bonds.

Of his father, Luther Hodges Jr. declares, "I have never seen him make a mistake." Although that sounds like praise, the son gave further explanation. "That isn't to say he might not have made mistakes early in his life. But I didn't see them because I was born in 1936 when he was 38 years old, and I knew him then as an efficient manager of business and government."

Stressing the expectation of his father that one must always do well, Luther Hodges Jr. says he is himself something of a rebel. But the rebellion is almost affectionate in its father-son relationship. "He is punctual to a fault," said Luther Jr. "I am just the opposite. I am usually late everywhere I go."

Martha Hodges objects some of the time, likewise, to punctuality and efficiency. "You have missed many good times by always being on time," she once told her husband.

Martha and Luther Hodges pin the bars on Ensign Luther Hodges Jr. when he was graduated from the University of North Carolina in 1957 and was commissioned in the U. S. Naval Reserve.

But his wife and children agree that Luther Hodges is sentimental and that he is idealistic. His life at home is like clockwork, just as at the office— 6:30 a.m. rising time ("But I usually beat him up," said Mrs. Hodges) exercise daily, no smoking, and early to bed.

When he first became Governor he said to his doctor, William Dewar of Raleigh, "I want you to be my physician in the Chinese tradition. I don't want to have to call you after I became ill. I want you to watch me before I get sick. Check me over from time to time. Maybe this is preventive medicine. But I don't have time to be ill." Dr. Dewar did just that. He prescribed little more than vitamins, and the regimen that the governor had been following for years anyhow. During the Hodges' two years of filling the unexpired Umstead term, and the four-year term from 1956 to 1960, he didn't miss a day's work and seldom had anything beyond a slight sniffle. Two or three times a week a masseur from the Raleigh YMCA came to the Mansion and gave the Governor an invigorating massage. It was a part of the good health regimen.

Life magazine featured Governor Hodges in a saucy pictorial display about North Carolina's hunt for new industry. The **Life** photographers even enticed the governor to promote some of the state's textiles—namely, men's undergarments and a wrinkle-proof suit in which the Gov. was shown in the shower. It was for North Carolina and the rising per capita wealth of its people! He had a passion to help his state!

In endeavoring to raise standards of living for North Carolina's 4½ million people, Governor Hodges tried twice—first unsuccessfully in 1957, and again (successfully) in 1959—to get the General Assembly to adopt a minimum wage law in the state, the first in the South!

He made another vital move for improving the state's revenues and services to the people by influencing the legislature to adopt a withholding tax for the state, similar to federal tax withholding.

Governor Hodges also learned to be courteous and discreet, if not always fully cooperative, with politicians. He came to have respect for politics and its participants, and he remained a strict party man. "If things are wrong with the Methodist Church, I do not leave the Methodist Church and join another church," said Luther. "I try to make changes within the Methodist Church. And if I feel that it is time for changes or renovations within the Democratic party, I don't join the Republican Party, or some other party. I try to exert influence to change the things I think may be wrong inside the Democratic Party. But I remain a Democrat."

Since the day when he made many state appointments without consulting county chairmen, Governor Hodges had mellowed in his views towards politicians—even though at a cordial and polite distance. He explained:

> I made it a strict point to select people for the various boards and commissions, old and new, based on fitness, ability, and dedication to state service. My philosophy in appointments

was that, all things being equal, I would generally appoint people active in the Democratic
Party. I did not reward party workers or
friends unless they were qualified. I only appointed those I felt to be of the highest caliber—
men and women who would do the best job for
North Carolina.

Paul Johnston and others can underscore the
Hodges policy of fairness and determination not to
exert official power and influence in behalf of a
man because he was a relative or friend—nor just
because he had once worked for him. Towards the
end of the Hodges administration, a friend was talking to Paul Johnston about his future, and Johnston
told him he didn't know yet what his future career
would be.

"You have nothing to worry about," said the
friend lightly. "Governor Hodges will take care of
you."

"If you think that," said Johnston, "you don't
know Governor Hodges. He wouldn't lift a finger.
I'll be looking for a job on my own, and I like it
that way."

Another acquaintance who knows Governor
Hodges well said, "A stranger who comes in off the
street and asks for a job, or an appointment in government, would stand a better chance of getting it
than a man who has worked for the governor or
who is a friend or relative. He's rigid about this
matter of no conflict of interests, and he hews to it
down the line."

Hugh Morton, who helped Governor Hodges in
his campaign for the full term, undergirds that im-

pression. "I once asked him to help me out on a Grandfather Mountain project—something I thought could be done fairly, justifiably. But I got turned down flat. He's not one of these 'you-scratch-my-back-and-I'll-scratch-yours' men." Both Johnston and Morton say these things admiringly.

One day Paul Johnston popped into the governor's office and he was smiling. He said, "Governor, I've just had an interesting telephone conversation with a man from New Jersey." He said, "I'm Senator So-and-So from the State Senate of New Jersey, and I was traveling in your state of North Carolina on U. S. 301 going North beyond Rocky Mount, and one of your patrolmen gave me a ticket. I'm just calling you to tell you to have Governor Hodges fix it for me!"

Johnston tried to explain and said, "This isn't the kind of thing we do in North Carolina."

The man said, "I said for you to ask Governor Hodges if he wouldn't handle this for me because I'm Senator So-and-So."

Paul said, "If you'll let me open the door leading to his office and hear me tell him, you can hear the explosion."

The man changed his mind about talking with Governor Hodges. But Johnston, to make the turn-down more palatable, added, "Things like that are not done in this administration in North Carolina, and it's not done in North Carolina generally. You will be surprised to know, Senator, that we have a senior United States Senator who was given a ticket for speeding in North Carolina, and we have a congressman from North Carolina who was treated likewise, that the secretary of state, I believe it was, had the same experience, and the governor's own son was recently given a ticket for traveling thirty-five miles an hour in a twenty-mile speed zone."

Ralph Howland, a newspaperman when Hodges first became governor and later a public relations man for both the state and North Carolina industry, corroborates some of the "duty and impartiality" aspects noted by others associated with the governor. "He won't let you get obligated to him," said Howland, "and if he suddenly finds that he is in some way obligated, he'll pay you back in a hurry and in good measure, and often get you obligated to him in return." This is a continuation of the boyhood rule followed by Luther Hodges—"never to be beholden to anyone."

Martha Hodges presided over the Mansion with a practical hand. Her tastes and decisions and likes and dislikes were ordinarily similar to Luther's, but whereas Luther makes decisions quickly, she likes to talk things over. Martha also has an intuition that usually leads her to the right course of action. The Mansion is a public place as well as the governor's home, and about 5,000 to 6,000 people a year were entertained officially or semi-officially. Besides that, there were classes of school children and other groups who simply like to walk through the governor's home, as though visiting a museum. The Hodges retained some privacy by use of a schedule —visits by the public only during certain specific

Family portrait, 1957. Seated on sofa, left to right: Nancy Hodges Finlay, Gov. Hodges, Martha Hodges (holding Donald Bernard III) and Betsy Hodges Bernard. Seated on floor are Martha Bernard, Vivian Finlay, Vary Finlay, and Carol Bernard. Standing are John Finlay, Luther Hodges Jr., and Donald Bernard. This was taken at a family gathering in the Governor's mansion in Raleigh.

morning hours. If groups wanted to use the ground floor of the Mansion for a tea or similar gathering, they had to do it by appointment. The Hodges family lived upstairs, and there was sufficient privacy, seven rooms and seven baths—enough for official and personal visitors.

A custom of breakfasts for legislators was established. Governor Hodges invited two dozen or so members of the General Assembly at a time to come to the Mansion for a North Carolina breakfast. Legislators were reminded of the words to the song **Chattanooga Choo Choo:** "Dinner in the diner; nothing could be finer than to have your ham and eggs in North Carolina."

A day before one 1959 breakfast, Luther asked Martha what she was going to serve.

"Bacon and eggs," said Martha.

"I'd like you to serve country ham at this one." Addison Hewlett was the new speaker of the House of Representatives and would sit at the Governor's left. A more than substantial breakfast might swerve the speaker in favor of the Governor's legislative program. At least, it wouldn't hurt.

But Martha protested. "Luther, country ham is too expensive. We have to pay the bills ourselves."

"I know it's expensive," said Luther. "But the tradition at these breakfasts is to serve ham. I think we ought to serve good North Carolina country ham."

"I knew she would serve the ham since I had requested it," wrote Hodges in **Businessman in the**

Wedding picture. Mr. and Mrs. Luther Hodges Jr., center, pose with Martha and Luther Hodges, left and right, at the wedding of Luther Jr. in 1958.

Statehouse, "but I was certainly not prepared for what happened at the breakfast."

As was the custom at the Mansion, the Governor was served first. Then the platter was carried to his right around the table. Hewlett, at his left, was the last to be served. Just as the platter reached Hewlett, the legislator before him took the last slice of ham. "I saw with horror that the plate was empty," said Luther Hodges. He said to the waiter, "Clarence, bring Mr. Hewlett some ham, quickly." Clarence hesitated and replied, "Governor, there ain't no more."

Luther found later that Martha had told the cook the governor had insisted on serving country ham, but she added that she wanted only twenty-eight pieces cooked. She didn't want any of the expensive ham wasted.

She hadn't counted on one representative's taking two slices of ham. That is what happened and why Speaker Hewlett had to do without. Amused legislators discussed the episode. The next morning ham was served again to a new party of legislators. This time there were eight slices left over. Mrs. Hodges wasn't taking any chances of running short. One freshman legislator asked the governor, "Can I go back into the kitchen?"

"Why?" asked Governor Hodges.

"I want to get some ham for Add Hewlett," said the legislator. Everyone laughed. The legislator wrapped up some ham and presented it on the floor of the House to the Speaker, with a flourish and appropriate oratory.

A page delivering the ham capped the climax. He fell sprawling and the ham ended up on the floor.

"I was surprised that my administration got as much legislation approved by the House in that session as it did," said Governor Hodges.

Christmas time in the Mansion was memorable. Luther Jr. came over from Chapel Hill, and the two daughters came with their families. Luther described it:

"Betsy, who lived out in the state of Washington, came with her husband and three children, and on occcasion we had Nancy come from Rangoon, Burma, with her British husband and three children. This was great fun. We always observed the ritual of the Christmas tree and the hanging of stockings. While in the Mansion, we continued a Christmas morning practice started in our home in Leaksville in 1922. The whole family would get together at the head of the stairs, march down to the Christmas tree, and open the presents from the stockings only. After breakfast, we came back to the tree and opened the gifts under it. We had a wonderful time.

"During the time we were in the Mansion, we had another ceremony every Christmas Eve night. At this one we would get together all the servants in the mansion, including the full-time employees and the prisoners on duty in the Mansion during the day. This ceremony with the present and former prisoners was a tree ceremony, and occasionally we would bring in a preacher who would talk for a few minutes and lead us in prayer. At other times we would do it ourselves. There would be singing on the part of the prisoners, and then gifts would be exchanged. Each servant usually received from six to ten gifts."

Chapter Sixteen

From Raleigh to Washington

As he prepared to leave the Mansion after six years in Raleigh, Luther Hodges reviewed the finished and unfinished business of the state. Typically, he began to scan and audit the job itself. How can a future governor give better service and leadership? What changes are feasible in the governorship of North Carolina so that a governor may better execute his duties and improve the processes of state government? What other executive and legislative improvements are advisable? "Looking Ahead" is the final chapter of **Businessman in the Statehouse** in which he frankly makes suggestions to legislators and to the people of North Carolina. These are:

1. The governor ought to be permitted to serve a second term. To do this the state constitution would have to be amended. A governor "does not have time in a single four-year period to get a full-fledged program more than just started."

2. The veto power should be given to the governor. North Carolina is the only state not granting its governor that authority.

3. The governor should be given decent office quarters. These in the Capitol building are cramped and undignified.

4. The General Assembly should consider meeting annually rather than once every two years.

5. Salaries of members of the Legislature should be raised.

6. The General Assembly ought to have a continuing legislative committee to operate with specified authority during the period when the Legislature is not in session.

7. More emphasis should be placed on the office of lieutenant governor.

8. The state ought to have a "short ballot"— that is, the governor should appoint many officials now elected. The appointments should be subject to legislative approval. Exceptions: the attorney general, auditor and treasurer should be elected.

9. The state should continue the process of reorganizing agencies of state government, to avoid duplications and promote efficiency.

10. Better salaries for teachers and better teachers are necessary. In addition to the minimum state salary level, the 174 local school districts of the state should supplement teachers' salaries to give quality to education. This should be done on a merit basis.

11. More attention should be devoted to long-range planning: in higher education and industry development. This could lead to a more balanced economy and greater per capita income. Agricultural diversification, more economic opportunity for Negroes, high standards of wages

Fishing in Montana, 1960.

and working conditions for labor, care for the deserving on public welfare, and better health care require attention. A scrutiny of the local and state tax structures is advisable. Improvements should be consistent in maintaining roads and highways. Where there is "a tremendous amount of out-of-state traffic," toll roads ought to be considered.

"I felt a touch of sadness that January day in 1961 when I took the carnation off my lapel for the last time," said Hodges. "For eight years, I had never been without a white carnation on my lapel, unless it was brushed off. After my trip to Russia in 1959, I received letters from various parts of the world asking where I got a white carnation in Russia. Well, in the Soviet Union I used an artificial one, as I did on other rare occasions. After turning over the keys to the Mansion and the Great Seal of the State of North Carolina to my successor, I took off the white carnation, never to wear one again. As it had become to many Tar Heels the symbol of my administration, so had the white carnation become a symbol to me of the faith in the future and service to the present that North Carolinians everywhere were willing to give their state."

Democratic Presidential candidate John F. Kennedy visited in the governor's Mansion in Raleigh in 1960. JFK and Hodges "hit it off well," as they say in North Carolina. Due at a public meeting on one occasion the punctual governor of North Carolina tensely glanced at his watch as the time slipped by while Senator Kennedy took his time in the shower. Hodges took a great interest in the 1960

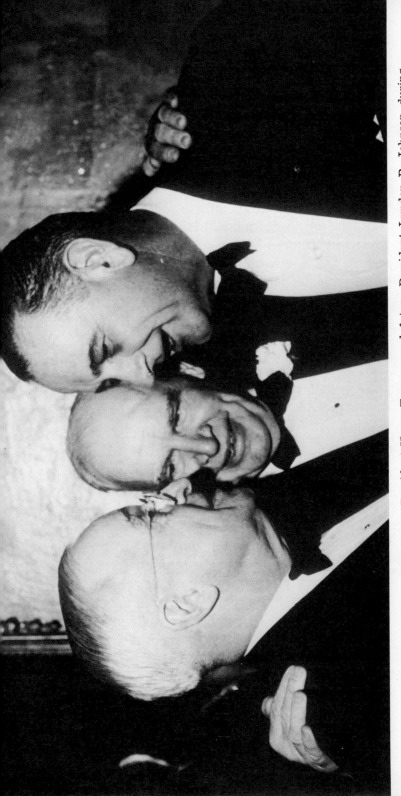

Gov. Hodges, center, with former President Harry Truman and future President Lyndon B. Johnson during campaign of 1960.

national campaign. "Like most of the North Carolina delegation to the Democratic National Convention in Los Angeles and most of the delegations of the southern states, I was for Senator Lyndon Johnson of Texas," he said. Hodges felt that it would be good to have a southerner in the White House, that there was unjust prejudice against a southerner, and that was bad for the country. LBJ would make a good President, Hodges believed. His election would help restore the South to a position of greater influence in national leadership—also good for the country. "Senator Kennedy knew how I felt and respected my point of view," said Luther. After Kennedy was nominated, Hodges, as he had told Mr. Kennedy he would, worked for him, made speeches, held press conferences from Pennsylvania to Texas. He put most of his energy on two questions: Kennedy's attitude towards business and the issue of religion. The Democratic Party then asked Hodges to do another thing in behalf of the Kennedy-Johnson ticket: to head a national committee of business and professional men. The committee was "moderately successful" admitted Hodges.

On the day before the 1960 elections, Governor Hodges was in Chapel Hill, presiding at a meeting of the University of North Carolina Board of trustees executive committee of which he was chairman. An aide whispered that a phone call from Washington, D.C. awaited him. It was Robert Kennedy. "Governor, would you mind monitoring Mr. Nixon's all-afternoon talkathon today?" he said. "He is talking from Detroit for several hours and we would like to have you answer it on a statewide broadcast."

President John F. Kennedy, left, with Governor Hodges, was soon to name Hodges Secretary of Commerce, 1960.

"I will enjoy doing that," said Hodges. He immediately gave orders to set up the monitoring procedure and to make arrangements for a broadcast. Then he returned to the trustees meeting.

About noon another call came, again from Robert Kennedy, who said, "Jack said he would sure like to have you appear with him on his television program tonight at Manchester, New Hampshire. It's at 6 o'clock."

"What should I do about monitoring the Nixon talkathon?" asked the governor.

Robert Kennedy replied in a most casual tone, "Jack said he would sort of like to have you do this, (the New Hampshire meeting) and I believe it will be important for you to do." He said there would be two programs, one with John F. Kennedy and Hodges, and another with the candidate, Gov. Hodges and two of the Kennedy sisters, and it was apparent the assignment had top priority over and above listening to the Nixon talkathon. "I don't know what the programs will be about," said Bobby Kennedy, "but he would like to have you here."

"All right, I'll be there," said Gov. Hodges.

"We can arrange for your transportation," said Bobby.

"That won't be necessary," said Hodges. "I'll take care of it from here, and come on my own."

University trustee Watts Hill began scouting around for a plane. He finally located Omar Dodson, pilot for Ed Richards of Raleigh. Omar flew the governor to New Hampshire and Hodges arrived at the television station at one minute to six, just as Senator Kennedy himself walked in the front door. Hodges, Kennedy and Pierre Salinger put their heads together. No format had been set. "Let's talk on broad subjects," said Kennedy.

"How about my asking you some questions about unemployment?" said Gov. Hodges. "I could suggest that some people are working less than forty hours a week, and they still have to pay high prices for groceries."

Kennedy said that was fine. "We can talk down to earth," he said.

The telecast was effective and a vote-getter, especially in the South. In the second program, Kennedy's three sisters asked the candidate questions in a casual, cozy style, and he answered them. "I would chime in from time to time," said Luther.

On December 2, 1960, after the Kennedy victory, Gov. Hodges was presiding in an intergovernmental relations meeting, again held in Chapel Hill, when a call came from the President-elect. JFK asked Hodges if he would come to Palm Beach the next morning at 10 o'clock. He didn't say what he wanted. Gov. Hodges took a train, to make sure of being on time. Punctual Luther didn't intend to be late for this appointment. But fate decreed that there would be a derailment on the Seaboard Air Line Railroad that night, delaying the train over an hour. "I am always on time, but that time I was an hour late for one of the most important events of my life," said Luther Hodges. When he arrived at the Kennedy home, he was astonished to find no one in the living room. He looked around and found Steve Smith and his wife, one of the Kennedy sisters, having coffee. They offered the governor a cup. A few minutes later Jack Kennedy looked in the door from another room and said, "Hey, Governor, I didn't know you were here."

"I probably showed surprise because I thought they were as concerned about my being late as I was concerned about not being there on time," said Luther. "But I found the Kennedys are very casual. Nothing seems to disturb them. They readily adapt themselves to any situation. It was a good thing to learn."

Kennedy and Gov. Hodges talked about ten minutes. Hodges was offered the job of Secretary of Commerce. It was the second appointment the President-elect had made to his Cabinet. They discussed the job, and Hodges accepted. In the press conference announcing the appointment, President Kennedy "charged Hodges with an accelerated growth of the American economy." Hodges made a statement pledging "to stimulate foreign trade and seek 'a new birth of confidence' in American business."

A national business writer observed that Secretary Hodges "faces one of the most ticklish problems: to come up with ways of helping to ease the balance of payments crisis. The outflow of dollars from the United States exceeds the inflow of foreign currencies and has caused a worrisome problem of loss of gold that has hurt the country overseas both economically and politically." Another commentator

Luther Hodges, world president of the Rotary Club movement (center), meets some of the child patients at Mengo Hospital after opening a clinic for spastic children, which has been built for the hospital by the Kampala Rotary Club. R. J. Mehta, president of the club, is in the left background.

observed what Hodges had done for North Carolina. "In 1958 when the nation invested 17.4 less in new industrial facilities, North Carolina registered a 35 percent increase," he wrote. "New jobs and payrolls have mushroomed there. He led a mission to 27 cities in six European countries to drum up business for North Carolina seaports, to interest foreign firms in locating in the Tar Heel State, and to get foreign licensing and franchise agreements for its firms."

Martha Hodges was quoted in an interview:

> I have mixed emotions. I hate for Luther to tackle another job. I had hoped he would retire and write a book. But he has always loved a good challenge. The country is in a crucial time and we need strong leadership. I know Luther wants to do what he can to help out.

The entire Hodges family was featured in the press. Betsy Hodges Bernard was interviewed by the newspaper in Anacortes, Washington, where she was living in 1960. "My daddy is a tough man," said Betsy. "He's not ugly tough, but he is tough."

In another formal announcement about the goals of the nation relating to the Commerce Department, President Kennedy added, "At a time when the strength and accelerated growth of the American economy is vital to our own prosperity and to fulfill our commitments to the cause of world freedom, the Department of Commerce has become one of the most important agencies of the government. Employing more than 36,000 people, Commerce will spend more than 500 million dollars this year to carry out its many functions."

The New Frontier, as the Kennedy regime became known, emphasized the youthful spirit of the new administration. It was stated that JFK is "the first President to be born in this century." So much was made of the 20th century birthdates of the new administration (Luther Hodges was the only one in the Kennedy Cabinet born in the 19th Century—1898) that before a Senate Committee he made a rejoinder. "Yes, but I am the only member of the Cabinet who drives a Thunderbird." After that first morning, and after looking over one of the big two-block-long buildings of the Commerce Department, the Secretary said to his personnel man, "I'd like to meet all the employees and talk to them." The man said that would be next to impossible, with the tremendous size, large number of employees and departments, scattered in over a dozen places in Washington—and over the country. "But I mean that," said Hodges. "I want to meet them and speak to them. Arrange for it. I'll talk to gatherings of Commerce employees wherever they are. Those I can't see personally I'll reach with a taped message."

Within two days Secretary Hodges had spoken to large audiences of Commerce workers, and covered the balance of the 36,000 by recorded messages. He carried around a handbook of the organization of the Commerce Department, and he began to study the many-sided agency.

The large department was made up of diverse components, some of them not obviously related to the business or commerce function. Some had called it "a dumping ground of agencies" meaning that in the growth of the federal government that many small and growing agencies had been put in Commerce because there didn't seem to be any other logical place to assign them. That was one reason why there was a cropping of rumors that agencies would soon break away from Commerce, or other departments of government would take them away from Secretary Hodges. The new Secretary was aware of eyes cast on his agencies and he took steps immediately to protect them. He recognized that Commerce was the "attic of agencies," but he didn't want to relinquish any of them until he had investigated their activities and functions and found out what they could contribute to the people's government where they were, or why they would be better off somewhere else. Hodges first went about mastering his job.

He asked Paul Johnston and Bob Giles to come to Washington. Johnston, his Department of Administration chief in Raleigh, became administrative secretary and took part in a gradual reorganization of Commerce. Giles became general counsel for the Commerce Department. The revitalization took place over several months. Prior to 1961, the Secretary of Commerce had twenty staff members reporting to him directly. Coordination of the agencies was minimal. Johnston proceeded to reorganize the department in a "line" rather than a "staff" manner. This meant that the many agencies of Commerce would be formed into groups, and there was an assistant secretary of Commerce to head each group. The seven major areas were Transportation, International Trade, Domestic Trade, Science and Technology, Economic Affairs and Economic Development. Under these were the Patent Office, Bureau of Standards, Bureau of Roads, Coast and Geodetic Survey, Maritime Administration, Weather Bureau, Census Bureau, Office of the Bureau of Economics, St. Lawrence Seaway Development, General Accounting Office, and others.

As the internal reorganization progressed, Secretary Hodges also focused his attention on foreign trade to achieve a better balance between imports and exports. This applied to western hemisphere trade as well as overall world trade. In a speech in Mexico City at the Third Inter-American Management Conference, Hodges spoke of the Alliance for Progress—between the United States and the Central and South American nations. He described goals for an increase in foreign investment to stimulate production and distribution, raising purchasing power and improve living standards. He pledged the cooperation of the United States government toward that end.

On the domestic front, Secretary Hodges developed programs for depressed areas of the United States called Area Development Administration. There was talk of establishing an independent agency of government to deal with these problems, but Congress authorized it for the Commerce Department.

The Secretary became sold on the idea that there could be a better balance of tourists between the United States and the rest of the world. Instead of

Americans spending hundreds of million of dollars a year abroad without any comparable amount of spending by people from Europe, for example, coming to spend vacations in this country, Hodges proposed to beckon to people of foreign lands to become tourists in America. He set up the U. S. Travel Service by authority of Congress. U. S. travel bureaus were established in key cities of the world. A stated purpose: "To induce foreigners to do their sightseeing in the U. S." It was a good will adventure as well as an economic investment. At the same time Hodges studied a possible cut on the $500 duty-free import allowance for American tourists overseas.

After Hodges had been in office only one month, the Associated Press published a report on the Secretary's activities:

1. He increased the number of U. S. trade missions abroad.

2. He made plans for more foreign visitors to this country.

3. He represented the President in talking to Congressmen on the nation's business problems.

4. He had seen and addressed some 12,000 Commerce employees.

5. He met daily with other top people in government to get in gear with the "New Frontier" total program.

6. He had advanced $100 million to the states to keep the road programs going.

7. He proposed to set up a science and technology program in the Department of Com-

merce to help business meet foreign competition.

8. He investigated what kinds of industries are appropriate and may be required to build up depressed areas.

9. He worked with the State Department and the Foreign Service Bureau to obtain better commercial reports that would be useful to business.

Chapter Seventeen

The Trade Expansion Act

A reporter asked the new Secretary of Commerce, "Are you a free trader or a protectionist?"

It was Secretary's Hodges first press conference, January 26, 1961.

Hodges smiled and replied, "I lean toward the side of greater international trade both ways. We can't export in greater volume without expecting to have a relative amount of imports coming in." **The Washington Post** reporter who had asked the question commented that the Secretary's answer sounded like the "classic explanation of the case of free trade."

The Washington press corps covered closely the Commerce Department and Secretary Hodges' activities, and he was equally communicative with the newsmen. It became apparent early that Hodges looked upon the news media as a prime opportunity to stay in touch with the American people. When threats loomed to whittle away some of his Commerce agencies, the **New York Daily News** said editorially: "Luther H. Hodges pooh-poohs the proposal that a new Department of Transportation be set up. Such a department, says Mr. Hodges, would cost a lot of money, make a lot of new federal jobs, and do nothing that can't be done satisfactorily by the Department of Commerce and the Interstate Commerce Commission. Somehow, we think we're going to like Secretary Hodges."

The **New York Herald-Tribune** headlined February 25, 1961: "Hodges Aims At Jobs, Not Boondoggle." The Secretary urged the House subcommittee on banking to "swift action on President Kennedy's $390 million depressed areas program." The idea was to engender reemployment in both urban and rural areas that suffer from chronic unemployment. Hodges assured the Congressmen that the purpose was not to take industry away from prosperous areas in order to pump it into ailing sections—but rather, to expand business and employment overall and give special attention to the industry potential of the depressed areas. The **New York Times** reported February 28, 1961, that President Kennedy was asking Congress to levy higher taxes on the trucking industry to pay their fair share of the $37 billion dollar interstate superhighway system to be completed by 1972. The President revealed information furnished to him by Commerce Department's Bureau of Public Roads that the heavier trucks ought to pay more of their share of the highway bill.

Of the recession that the nation experienced in 1961, Secretary Hodges sounded a hopeful note in

March. "I think we've hit the bottom," said Hodges. The Wall Street Journal quoted him saying the economy is ready to begin an upturn. "I think we can start from here and move up," said Hodges.

In response to commentators who conjectured whether the Kennedy Administration was "friendly to business or was anti-business," the Commerce Chief told steel manufacturers assembled in New York City on May 25 that the Kennedy administration was neither "a businessman's government" nor "anti-business." Instead, said Hodges, the administration is "committed to the support of the private enterprise system, a sound currency and a relationship with business marked not by antagonism and suspicion, but by respectful understanding and fruitful collaboration."

In the effort to get more travelers from Europe and other foreign nations to be tourists in the United States, the Buffalo, N.Y. **Evening News** quoted him in June. "Hodges Suggests Pretty Girls Greet Travelers to U. S." was the headline. "It wouldn't hurt to have a few pretty girls around that speak two or three languages that make people feel at home instead of having some guy who looks at you pretty tough and says, 'Let's see inside your bag'."

Hodges brought Voit Gilmore of Southern Pines, N. C. to Washington to head the U. S. Travel Service, and Gilmore, a natural promoter and enthusiast, got tourist traveling rolling. Delegations from American states were encourage to go to Europe and put out a welcoming mat that would stretch all the way across the Atlantic. A North Carolina contingent was

one of the first to visit London. Charles B. Wade
Jr. of Winston-Salem said in a press interview in
London, "Our first impression after hearing this
briefing is that there is a greater potential for
British travel to North Carolina than we ever im-
agined."

It was in March 1962, that the press reported
Luther Hodges' most formidable assignment of the
Kennedy Administration. The **New York Herald-
Tribune** headline expressed it: "Hodges Takes Front
Rank in U. S. Trade Promotion." An account of the
emergence was expressed by United Press International: "The Department of Commerce, in the first
14 months of the Kennedy administration, has moved
into the front rank in the nation's foreign trade relations. The man primarily responsible is Secretary
Luther H. Hodges, former Governor of North Carolina who has shown more get up and go than any
of his Cabinet predecessors since Herbert Hoover . . .
He has also taken on big responsibilities in propping
up national economic growth and toward fostering
good will toward the Kennedy administration in the
business community."

President Kennedy had indeed assigned primary
responsibility to Luther Hodges in getting his Trade
Expansion Act approved by the Congress. Hodges
devoted his main attention to the bill. Much was at
stake. The nation's Reciprocal Trade Agreement program was about to expire. The Kennedy Trade Expansion Act was needed to take its place in order to
continue the policies of free trade. In a speech in
Baltimore, Hodges put the matter in perspective:

Probably the most important piece of legislation awaiting action today is the Trade Expansion Act, which gives the President power to negotiate for freer trade in an expanding world economy.

This act is vital to our export expansion program to deal with our continuing balance of payments problems. It is essential to prevent the development of the European Common Market and other trade blocs in an atmosphere of protectionism. It is indispensable as a means of avoiding an economic split between Western Europe and the U. S.—a split that would shatter our political unity and delight the Communists.

In another speech June 4, 1962, addressing the Rotary International Convention in Los Angeles, Hodges said this of the Kennedy program:

Trade is an essential building block—not only for its diffusion of material goods, and its contribution to higher living standards, but for its power to bring together the lives of people at innumerable points of contact. If men are ever to think of themselves as brothers, they must begin by acting as neighbors—talking civilly, dealing candidly, and accepting without astonishment, the natural difference between them.

In another Los Angeles speech, Hodges said:

Under the provisions of the legislation before Congress, the President would be given authority to reduce tariffs by 50 percent on most products and more on certain items sold to the Common Market . . . The Trade Expansion Act does not automatically cut tariffs for us. It is merely an instrument by which we will be able to gain a competitive edge for our products in return for concessions for foreign goods shipped here.

America must realize that the soft, easy days of order-taking that followed the war are over. Americans must shed their flab and return to lean, hard-muscled selling, both at home and abroad.

When Congress finally approved the Trade Expansion Bill in the summer of 1962, the margin was substantial, 298 to 125 in the House. But after the bill was finally passed, Secretary Hodges was only beginning his promotion and salesmanship. "This new Trade Act **assures** us of absolutely nothing," he said. "It **offers** no more than an opportunity to meet a changing world, as it is and will be. Unless it is implemented, wisely and effectively, it is merely a new acquisition for the Library of Congress . . . The potential for increased trade is tremendous."

Hodges listed seven working areas by which the 1963 economy could be improved:

1. Development of the habit of cooperation—between management and labor, and between business and government.
2. Cut personal income taxes and corporate taxes; it will spur economic growth.
3. Develop new and improved consumer products.
4. Sell more American goods abroad.
5. Sell more aggressively at home.
6. Help educate the American people on the economic facts of life.
7. Adjust our thinking to the broad problems of global markets, global investment oppor-

tunities, and the global economic challenge of the Sino-Soviet bloc.

Many political and economic observers believe that one of President Kennedy's main achievements was the passage of the Trade Expansion Act. It was certainly the top-priority bill of the JFK administration. It was a victory for Kennedy, a victory for the United States, a victory for world trade.

To Luther Hodges, the attainment of his nation's and his President's objective gave him one of his greatest thrills of personal satisfaction.

Hodges worked diligently at increasing U. S. exports of goods and services and made hundreds of contacts and speeches to inspire U. S. businessmen to sell abroad. By the end of his term the excess of exports over imports approached six billion dollars.

Jim Morton, Secretary Hodges' press secretary, called his boss "the apostle of foreign trade." Hodges was bold and frank and quick in his missionary promotion of trade and competition, Morton learned. "This was very much a part of his convictions about the value of the private enterprise economic system," said Morton. "He was ideally geared to become the nation's chief economic spokesman for free enterprise. He lived the American Dream, and he saw through his own experiences what made that dream a reality. He went about with an evangelical zeal to show how that system works."

Luther Hodges held more press conferences than any other Cabinet member, His main idea was to communicate and he knew he could reach large numbers of people and his specific publics by telling his story to mass audiences, Morton disclosed. "His wit and his capacity to come up with a well-turned phrase endeared him to the press," said Morton.

Morton also noticed that Luther Hodges "notices what is relevant." "Once we took an eight day trip into eight South American countries, travelling day and night. I observed then how Secretary Hodges set his priorities on time and the importance of the tasks to be done. He wasted no time. When he began his conversation with the President of Colombia in Bogota, he went straight to the point. He said the practice of barter agreements, practiced by Colombia, penalized competition, and he had the Colombian President agreeing in principle.

Luther Hodges could invite the Japanese to invest in plants in the United States because he had confidence in the system of free enterprise and free competition. "He believes we can invest in Japanese industry and they can invest in ours, with benefit to both," said Morton. On one occasion a party of top Russian trade officials called on Secretary Hodges. In the midst of business conversations, Hodges said, "I have a gift for you." He took a package from a desk. "These are elastic shoe laces," he said. "They were made in my home state of North Carolina. These shoe laces can be a symbol of cooperation for as you grow more flexible in your attitudes and practices you may even be able to keep your own shoe laces tied without any bending at all."

The Russians laughed and accepted the elastic shoe laces with thanks.

Chapter Eighteen

Revitalization

To keep the pipe line of communications open between the huge Commerce Department and the American people, Secretary Hodges gave primacy to his information assistants. William Ruder, who served during 1961 and 1962, and Jim Morton, who came in 1963 and stayed through the Hodges administration, were members of his top staff and participated in the inner councils of policy-making and the decisions and their implementation which radiated out over the world. Few Cabinet members in American history have had a better "press" than Luther Hodges. First it was because of his actions and his sincerity in carrying out the responsibilities of his office, and second, it was because of his open-door, freedom-of-information practices, that made the Department of Commerce known to the American public as it had never been known before.

He also stressed, time and again, use of plain and simple language. One anecdote he told, for which he claimed no authorship owing to the fact it had originally been told about one of his agencies, the Bureau of Standards, illustrated his avoidance of gobbledegook. The story:

A plumber with a limited command of English wrote to the Bureau of Standards. He said he had found that hydrochloric acid opened clogged drainage pipes in a hurry, and wanted to know if it was a good thing to use.

A bureau scientist wrote him back: "The efficacy of hydrochloric acid is indisputable, but the corrosive residue is incompatible with metallic permanence."

The plumber promptly wrote back thanking the scientist for telling him the method is all right. The scientist showed the letter to his boss, who got worried.

"We cannot assume," he wrote the plumber, "responsibility for the production of toxic and noxious residue with hydrochloric acid and suggest you use an alternative procedure."

The plumber promptly replied that the acid was working just dandy.

This letter was passed on to the boss' boss, who broke off the correspondence tersely:

"Don't use hydrochloric acid. It eats hell out of the pipes."

In a speech to the American Society of Newspaper Editors, Secretary Hodges said, "In a sense, the U. S. Department of Commerce is a great newspaper, issuing daily its vast output of fact for the information and guidance of the public and the nation in the conduct of their daily affairs and in their planning for the future." He added, "You couldn't make up your papers without help from the Commerce Department." And he proved it. "One of our reports makes your front page every day"—the weather forecasts by the U. S. Weather Bureau. He told them about the work of the Census Bureau. When people ask "How's business?", the newspapers and the Commerce Department have an answer, declared the Secretary. "We favor an open door policy with respect to the work we do," he said. Yet Hodges recognized the dangers of lubricating the free flow of information. "Will I put my foot in my mouth?" he asked rhetorically and to the editors, and he answered himself, "Possibly, but as a public official I can't duck behind a 'no comment' curtain."

A Scripps-Howard syndicate staff writer wrote:

Let's call in the governor! is a suggestion heard increasingly around the White House these days.

It means Commerce Secretary Luther Hodges—ex-governor of North Carolina—will be pulled into another conference on the business-economic side of running the government.

This is a change. Over the years, when big home-front executive decisions were made, the Commerce Department usually was left on the outside . . . Today it is gaining status. The energetic Mr. Hodges has needled some life into this huge, sprawling stepchild and seems on the way to giving it importance it has not had . . .

Secretary Hodges founded a new magazine, **International Commerce,** to boost foreign trade. It was distributed abroad. The 60-page weekly contained trade and business news gathered continuously by U. S. commercial attaches and foreign service officers in virtually every country and had feature articles and photographs. Advisories included export and import opportunities, investment potentials, trade trends, and information useful to new business development.

Giving his attention at the same time to the home markets, the Secretary set up in the Commerce Department a Business Service Center where businessmen can come and find out where they may go and get contracts, sales, and other essentials to their enterprise. Later a short-sighted committee chairman in Congress eliminated it.

Opponents of trade between the United States and the U.S.S.R. stress the contradiction of trading with Russia and making the Soviet Union stronger, when at the same time Russia is carrying on a cold war with the United States and providing war materials to nations who have engaged in active combat with U. S. troops. The same objection to trading with Communist nations was advanced when the United States troops were fighting in Korea. Since then, the same position has been voiced in objections to trade with the Russian bloc while Americans are fighting in Viet Nam.

Two years before he became Secretary of Commerce, Hodges had visited Russia and talked with Russian leaders, and he was convinced that, while the United States should not sell Russia materials for weapons or other strategic items, it could be a contribution to better understanding and mutuality of peaceful interests if there could be limited trade between Russia and the United States in goods that are not of war-making potential.

"We ought to be able to sell Russia anything they can eat, smoke or drink," said Secretary Hodges. Hodges reflected President Kennedy's position on trade, including the peaceful exchanges with the Communist bloc countries, and he set about expanding that import-export trade. One squabble arose when the United States was about to permit sales of a large amount of wheat to Russia. Trouble arose, not only because of the normal opposition to selling to a Communist country, but also due to difficulties involving the U. S. Maritime Commission. Not enough vessels were available to carry the wheat— at least not enough on ships that would be loaded by U. S. longshoremen. Russia got some of the wheat, but not all that was desired. Despite that, the Kennedy-Hodges view generally prevailed: that Russia could be sold anything that could be eaten, smoked or imbibed. Wheat was "something you ate." At a World Affairs Conference in Los Angeles, the Secretary said, "By denying basic flexibility, we would surrender in advance the opportunity to use trade as a weapon for peace and better understanding."

Every Tuesday morning from 8:30 to 9:30, Secretary Hodges met with his seven assistant secretaries and his immediate staff which included his administrative secretary, his Congressional liaison offcer, his press officer and his own personal deputy. After acquainting them with what the White House dis-

cussion had been, relative to Commerce, he told them
what the President "wants us to do." Sometimes
one of the assistant secretaries had a special report
to make of interest to all of them, even though Secretary Hodges usually had conferred individually with
each assistant secretary. Frequently Hodges asked
his assistants to help him prepare for inquiries that
might be made at impending press conferences. The
news conference was the prime way of acquainting
the people of the country about the nation's business.

"What kinds of questions will they ask me about
that road in Ohio?" Hodges asked Dan Martin,
Under-secretary for Transportation. Martin exer-
cised authority over the Bureau of Public Roads. "Do
they really have an electronic road, with a beacon
picking up a speeding car? What's our relation to the
project?"

Martin replied that about the only thing that
could be said is that the Ohio plan did seem to have
some merit, that the Bureau of Roads was negotiat-
ing on the matter, but was not ready for any con-
clusive decision. Hodges nodded and jotted a note
to himself, for later use.

The Secretary asked the Assistant Secretary for
Economic Affairs about potentialities for economic
growth for the next quarter. "Will the rate stand
up?" asked Hodges. "Do we need a tax cut?" Following one of these meetings Secretary Hodges asserted
to the press that a tax reduction is in order if the
strength of the economy is to be maintained.

To the assistant secretary for science and technology Hodges referred to a complaint from a man

applying for a patent. "It has already been three years since he applied and he doesn't have his patent yet. What's the problem?"

Assistant Secretary Herbert Hollemon replied, "We've really got a mess. We have a large backlog of patent applications. We are working on a way to use automation in meeting the heavy demand, investigating and testing."

The Secretary asked other query potentials. Jim Morton, the press officer, suggested a couple of likely questions, and Hodges relayed them to the assistant secretaries—and armed himself with answers.

Hodges became almost immediately concerned with the role of the nation's Business Advisory Council, an organization of big businessmen presumed to advise the Commerce Department. The BAC was composed of some of the most distinguished executives of industry, banking and other business. They met in executive session. No information ever reached the public on what they talked about, what the agenda was, and what conclusions had been reached. The Council met with high officials of the administration and with heads of regulatory agencies. But all discussions were closed to the press and public. This was wrong, thought the new Secretary of Commerce, and he was determined to take action on his official responsibility because the BAC had headquarters in the Commerce Department and had a nebulous tie-in with Commerce, but without Commerce's having any real say-so about its policies and practices.

Following a press conference, newspapers reported: "Commerce Secretary Luther H. Hodges gave the government's Business Advisory Council a stiff ultimatum: open up your meetings or quit."

Hodges, according to the news account, "delivered his warning in the gentlest of terms with a smile on his face. But the message came forth loud and clear. BAC is a self-perpetuating group of 174 executives from blue-chip corporations."

Hodges agreed with critics of the Council who complained that the closed-door huddles with key federal aides give members access to information not available to the public generally. He said the BAC would be obliged to do these things: (a) have no secret sessions, (b) admit small businessmen as well as big businessmen, (c) work on specific problems of the Commerce Department. The Hodges statement was made a short time after the chairman of the BAC, Ralph J. Cordiner of General Electric, had resigned from the Council following the electric machinery price scandals of 1960.

The Business Advisory Council balked at the Hodges proposals. They took their pleas for executive sessions to President Kennedy. The President, eager to maintain a friendly association between business and government, was torn between placating the BAC and standing behind Secretary Hodges. Meanwhile Roger Blough, president of U. S. Steel Co., became chairman of the Council. The upshot was BAC and Commerce agreed to sever their relationship. The Council continued to meet in closed session which it does to this day. BAC maintains a close relationship with the White House and the U. S. State Department. Jack Behrman, one of Hodges' assistant secretaries who became responsible for both foreign and domestic trade, said "Hodges was right. It was an unhealthy situation with 174 businessmen in the know about government policies and 50,000 businessmen not knowing." Behrman, now a professor of foreign trade at the University of North Carolina, declares that the critical issue remains: how business relates itself to and gives advice to government. "It has not been resolved to this day," said Behrman.

JFK leaned over backwards to cooperate with the business community, in one case too far. It was ironic that Roger Blough, who was largely instrumental in cutting the BAC tie with Commerce, overreached himself in his new confidence with Kennedy. To hold down inflation Kennedy thought he had reached an agreement with U. S. Steel not to raise prices. Government claimed it had got unions to settle for lesser wage increases in order to hold the lid on inflation. But despite this understanding, U. S. Steel in April, 1962, raised prices $6 a ton. Blough notified Kennedy of the action. The President flared up, demanded the steel price rise be rescinded. Secretary Hodges was quick to support Kennedy's outrage and concern. U. S. Steel, facing an outcry from press and public as well as the President, did not jump the price of steel after all. In his book **The Business Conscience**, written in 1963, following a speech on ethics in business at Columbia University, Hodges wrote:

I was convinced at the time, and still feel very strongly, that the behavior of the top officials of U. S. Steel was completely wrong under existing conditions. To put it bluntly, they misled the President and the public by withholding information or leaving the impression they were going along with the anti-inflation program outlined by the President.

During the many weeks of negotiations with the steel union, the corporation at no time informed the union or the government that it would increase prices even if the workers accepted a modest settlement. Mr. Blough had repeated opportunities to make this disclosure to the President, to Secretary of Labor Arthur Goldberg, to myself, or to union officials. He chose to remain silent. In my judgment, this silence was not honest for the following reasons:

Mr. Blough must have known that the government had only one purpose in urging the union to accept a modest settlement: it wanted to forestall an increase in steel prices. In fact, this was the chief justification for government interest in the negotiations.

By keeping silent, Mr. Blough misled the government so that, in effect, the steel industry could reap the benefits of official efforts to moderate the union's contract demands.

Luther Hodges, both a businessman and a leader in government, has become one of the world's foremost advocates of friendly human and business relationships. This implies leveling, straight talk, full information communicated, as well as the essential partnership between industry and government of the people. "The average businessman seems to have difficulty understanding and appreciating the role of government in the economy, or seeing the ethical side of relations between business and government," said Secretary Hodges. "The businessman who fails to do his duty to government is not ethical, any more than is the man who fails to do his duty to his family, neighbors and community."

Hodges told businessmen that there was much "careless thinking and careless talk" critical of government on the part of some businessmen. The fact is, said Hodges, "What is done by government is designed to help one segment of business against the harmful actions of another segment."

Secretary Hodges helped draw up a code of conduct for business. It was rather specific because Luther explained that "the code should avoid fuzzy platitudes and deal in plain language with the real problem areas. He proposed the following code:

1. We will strive at all times to conduct the affairs of this company to merit public confidence in American business and industry and faith in our free, private, competitive enterprise system.

2. We will see that our employees are given every opportunity to progress with the company and are appropriately compensated for their work.

3. We will deal fairly with customers and suppliers and extend to them the same treatment we wish to receive ourselves.

4. We will compete vigorously to serve our customers and expand our business, but will avoid unfair or unethical practices.

5. We will seek, through sound management practices, to produce the profit necessary to the continued progress of the business and so fulfill our responsibilities to our stockholders, employees, customers, community and nation.

President Kennedy supported Secretary Hodges in a new organization called the Business Ethics Advisory Council of the Department of Commerce. JFK said, "I think it would be very beneficial if business groups today would consider what they could do to protect themselves from charges of conflicts of interest of the kind we have recently seen." The President addressed the new Council formed by Hodges and sat in on an exchange of views, and asked questions throughout the meeting.

Luther Hodges worried that not enough Americans have a basic understanding of how the economy works. Too many Americans suffer, he said, from "economic illiteracy." The Department of Commerce published a booklet entitled "Do You Know Your Economic ABC's?" It was widely distributed and is a document of lasting benefit to people who do not understand the jargon normally employed by a professor of economics. In plain language understandable to the average man, the booklet explains how the free enterprise system works, including exposition of the fundamentals of supply and demand, the Gross National Product, wages and costs, and other basics of money, banking, and making ends meet. The price for a copy—20 cents. He said: "If ignorance paid dividends most Americans could make a fortune out of what they don't know about economics. How can we grow and prosper if our people are, to put it bluntly, economic boobs!"

The Secretary was a traveling salesman in Commerce, just as he had been a traveling North Carolina governor, selling North Carolina and its products. He visited the U. S. Foreign Travel bureaus all over the world, and attended international "Trade Fairs." In over 100,000 miles traveled in one year, he made 90 speeches, 62 of them prepared and the others off-the-cuff. He visited the 50 states, Mexico, Canada, Puerto Rico, Japan, West Germany, Spain, Belgium, the Netherlands and Finland.

A favorite occasional story going around the Washington rumor mills is that a Cabinet member, or other high officer is going to resign. The word made its way around Washington after the first few months that Luther Hodges was going to quit. It cropped up time and again for the four Hodges years under Presidents Johnson and Kennedy. Once a little boy from Durham, North Carolina, wrote to President Kennedy saying he'd heard "Secretary Hodges is going to be fired." The boy asked the President to say it wasn't so. JFK forwarded the letter to Hodges and asked him to reply to the boy in the President's behalf that he had "absolutely no intention of firing Secretary of Commerce Hodges." Luther passed the word along to the Durham youngster, and it was published in the papers. But the rumors persisted, as they do today about other Cabinet officers and other government officials.

In November 1963, Secretary Hodges and Mrs. Hodges, accompanied by five other Cabinet members and their wives, accepted an opportunity to fly to Tokyo for an inter-cabinet meeting between the United States and Japan. But as they flew across the Pacific, they learned that President John F. Kennedy had been assassinated in Dallas, Texas. The plane bearing the Cabinet members and their wives promptly turned around and came back to the United States. In his trip report to his family and friends, Luther said, "Martha and I are still numb as I suppose you are."

Secretary Hodges had respect and admiration for President Kennedy. The two got along well from the beginning. Hodges admired JFK, not only for his leadership and vision, but for his manner, his communications ability, his grasp of world affairs and his courage. Luther also was impressed by the family life of the Kennedys—the whole Kennedy tribe. He liked the feeling of family loyalty, getting together, cooperativeness, the all for one and one for all kind of togetherness. He once said to Luther Jr., "Let's be more like the Kennedys."

Although Hodges had been a Lyndon Johnson man before and during the Democratic National Convention of 1960, he had become an indefatigable member of Kennedy's New Frontier and its ideals. Kennedy's death left him shaken. But like other Americans and like the new President Johnson himself and others in government, Luther Hodges again plunged into his work of business and government— under a new leader and amid new crises and steady economic upsurge in the United States.

Chapter Nineteen

"Business Is Almost Too Good"

Trade! Trade! Trade! Sell! Sell! Sell Keep moving and producing! Insist on quality! Hire men and keep them employed! Pay attention to research! Find out new ways of doing things! Automate! Advertise! Tell your story! Watch the income and outgo! Don't waste! Work! Work! Work! Be honest! Be ethical! Make friends! Trade and sell and serve, and try to make a profit! Luther Hodges didn't put those words in just that sequence, but that was the meaning of his actions as the nation went into the new year, 1964, under President Lyndon B. Johnson.

On January 2, 1964, only a month and a half after President Kennedy's assassination, the Secretary of Commerce received this message from LBJ:

I am deeply grateful to you for your faith and support in the past six weeks. Our nation has weathered a tragic storm and emerged secure because you worked long and hard under trying circumstances.

Other trading weathervanes seemed to be blowing favorably. Luther was given the figures on the upswing in the tourist travel by foreigners who had come to the United States in the previous 24 months. Visitors from abroad pumped $450 million into the U. S. economy in the years 1962 and 1963. **The New York Times** reported on January 8 that "Secretary of Commerce Luther H. Hodges has issued new licenses for export of $50 million worth of surplus wheat to the Soviet bloc." In a speech L. H. H. took note of protectionist tendencies on the part of some Americans. "Cut out whining about imports and get to work selling U. S. products such as beef to other countries," he said. "Product quality and imaginative merchandising is what we need. We have not yet licked the problem of agricultural commodities in the Common Market. Americans are going to have to get up off whatever we're sitting on and sell goods!"

Early in 1964 political talk began about the Presidential nominations and elections. It was universally accepted that President Johnson would be the Presidential candidate on the Democratic ticket. But the vice presidency was the subject of conjecture. With many others, Luther Hodges was mentioned. One commentator remarked that Hodges was being considered. Another commentator remarked that Hodges was "the only genuine Johnson man in the Cabinet." In 1960 Luther had told Bobby Kennedy "I'm all out for LBJ." At a press conference, when he was asked about the vice presidential speculations, Hodges quashed them. "It wouldn't be realistic to have two southerners on the ticket," he said. He thus eliminated his name as a running mate for LBJ in 1964.

Luther pitched into one of his favorite promotions—trade fairs where American goods were "in show cases." He personally attended fairs in Utrecht, Frankfurt, Paris, Barcelona, Zurich, Tel Aviv, Bari, Vienna, Helsinki, West Berlin, Stockholm and Dusseldorf.

His travel, his speeches, his press conference statements and his go-at-'em traits bolstered a spirit of confidence, not only in the nation but in Luther Hodges' own backyard—his staff and assistant secretaries and office associates in the Department of Commerce. Gerry Pratt, business editor of the Portland **Oregonian** said this: "When he is beyond earshot they talk of him as 'Big Luther,' not disparagingly at all, but with something of the affection of a sports fan for a baseball player when the ballplayer is hitting well. Luther Hodges has a good batting average today. He suggested the tax cut; he pumped our export business as one of the keys to straightening out the balance of payments, and our export business is up $4 billion or more; he sought a rapport between business and government, and perhaps never before has there been so much faith in the politicians."

His office staff surprised him on his 66th birthday March 9, 1964, and they spelled out their regard for him in this note signed by his secretary Peggy Tyler:

F is for the FIRE he lights beneath us
A is for the ALL we give
T is for the TRIPS we have to work on

H is for the HELL we get
E is for the ENERGY we use up
R is for the RIGHT he always is.

Put them all together, they spell FATHER, and
we love him more each day.

The recovery in the nation's economy that was
so noticeable in 1964 over the previous two years
was gratifying. But Secretary Hodges sounded a
warning. Speaking at a Florida World Trade Conference he said, "The nation's business is almost too
good." He said there must be an alert against price
rises. He cautioned against "excessive wage demands. These," said L.H.H., "could wreck the economy's upward spiral." He added: "If we are to compete abroad we must keep down the costs."

The fact that Hodges is a southerner, though
from a moderate and progressive state, often brought
the race question to the fore. Once Negro pickets
marched outside a hall where he was speaking. The
picketing was sparked by the fact the audience was
segregated. Hodges explained later that had he
known the hall was segregated he would not have
spoken there. As governor of North Carolina and
as Secretary of Commerce Hodges was scrupulously
fair in his race and employment policies and practices. Addressing an Alabama audience in 1964 he
said:

We are witnessing a social revolution center-
ing on the demands of Negro rights, and given
the whole history of the nation and of the world
itself, the ultimate outcome cannot be in doubt.

The Negro in America cannot be forever
denied equal opportunity and the full measure

of human dignity without the abandonment of everything America has stood for in the history of Western Civilization.

However, Hodges spoke out in opposition to violence and demonstrations that defy the law. "Hoodlums are harmful to the cause of Civil Rights," said L.H.H. "The Rights Act also does not mean that a job should be taken from one man in order to give that job to another."

An editorial writer speaking one day in praise of plain language and against technical economic jargon, used Luther Hodges as a splendid example. Asked at a press conference what were "the prospects" at a coming meeting on tariff negotiations, the Secretary of Commerce said, "We are guardedly optimistic." Then, said the writer, to show his disdain for gobbledegook, Hodges added, "That means they don't look very good." Editorial comment made was: "More plain speaking by higher-ups would humanize government and make it more understandable to the average person."

Moving from the Governor's Mansion in Raleigh to a home in Washington was not the only residential move made by Martha and Luther Hodges. They also bought a home in Chapel Hill, a large comfortable home in a secluded nook called "The Glen" just off the old main residential street of the University of North Carolina community. The house is on a promontory near the peak of the Chapel Hill plateau on a site overlooking the Triassic Basin. Ancient oaks, pine and hardwoods decorate the

front, and a tall persimmon tree stands at the walk-
way to the entrance.

As Luther had promised Martha in 1922 not long
after their marriage and on a trip to Chapel Hill,
"We will come back here to live some day." So they
established residence in Chapel Hill and in Washington. The Hodges flew down to Chapel Hill many
times during the 1961 to 1965 period, especially during holiday and vacation times, and many times the
family gathered there for their reunions.

In Washington Martha and Luther were a part
of the social life of the Capital expected of Cabinet
members and of other high officers of the Executive
and Legislative branches of the government. Martha
did her part and they entered into the protocol, the
diplomacy and the public relations aspects of official
Washington. Sometimes in interviews with press women, Martha was asked to compare her life in Washington with that in Raleigh. Although she valued
both experiences, she admitted finally that the years
in Raleigh were more satisfying because she, as
"First Lady" was able to do more things that were
worthwhile for the good of North Carolina people,
through cultural and civic and moral leadership in
ribbon cuttings, health and charity drives, campaigns for improvement of schools and help for the
underprivileged. She decorated the Mansion, represented Luther on occasions and "learned more about
government." Yet the time in Washington was "more
exciting," particularly in many of its national and
international overtones. The six years in Raleigh
were "more productive." Martha Hodges will answer

questions like that, but she wishes they wouldn't ask her to make comparisons.

While enjoying the whirl of Washington events, Luther clung to his early-to-bed rule. Once at a party given by Lord and Lady Caccia of Great Britain, the time was approaching 10 o'clock. Luther had known Lord and Lady Caccia even before he went to Washington. They had visited in North Carolina when Lord Caccia was ambassador from Britain to the United States. Luther said to Lady Caccia, "You know my habit of 10 p.m. curfew. Do you think it would be all right from the protocol standpoint if I leave in a few minutes?"

Lady Caccia registered mock horror. "Absolutely not" she laughed. "You must stay until the Princess goes home."

Luther laughed, too, and departed on the stroke of 10. On the way out of another reception a secret service man questioned him about leaving before the President did, and the Secretary of Commerce explained that the President is a younger man and keeps later hours.

Luther also took care of his health by his regular exercise and safety valve holiday excursions. In the summer of 1964 a newspaper reporter wrote of a small Tar Heel gathering at Atlantic City. Secretary Hodges was swimming with North Carolinians Tom Pearsall and Lunsford Crew, both of them members of the commission that had helped solve North Carolina's educational crisis eight years before. The reporter wrote: "A daredevil swimmer has been giving life guards here the jitters early every morning.

On Tuesday one of the guards was blowing his whistle until his face was red before the swimmer and two friends, far beyond the breakers, turned back toward shore. The swimmers were Secretary of Commerce Luther H. Hodges, 66, and his North Carolina friends Tom Pearsall and Lunsford Crew."

Aside from office conferences in Washington, Secretary Hodges often took his staff off for the weekend where they had a prolonged working seminar, sometimes at Camp David and sometimes at Quantico, Virginia. These usually lasted from Friday afternoon to Sunday morning. "There was plenty of time to go over big issues," said Jack Behrman, the international trade specialist. Behrman, who joined Hodges' staff about a month after the Secretary came into office, was teaching at the University of Delaware when he was interviewed for the job. At Behrman's request, Hodges released him when an opportunity came to teach at the University of North Carolina in 1964.

"Luther Hodges is a man you feel has a personal interest in the organization in which he is active," said Prof. Behrman. "He's on top of his job and he's committed wholly to what he is doing, as the most important factor of his day. He expects others to feel that same commitment. He expects you to be on top of **your** job. He expects an assignment to be carried out in a minimum time period, no dragging around, no bureaucratic higgling and haggling. With distinguished visitors he devotes plenty of time, and makes them feel that he has all the time in the world to devote to their interests. But even then he doesn't fool around. When a twenty minute appointment is up, it's up. He is not a dictator. He doesn't say 'you do it my way, bang, bang.' He wants to see and hear things simply and directly. You must have the froth cut away from the issue. Much is accomplished in staff meetings, but even more in man-to-man conferences. I would say to him, 'I've got a sheaf of problems.' He would reply 'All right, make an appointment.' We would meet and go over them one at a time, and invariably the decisions were made on the spot. One of his main achievements was his putting through the nation's Trade Expansion Act. It was the only important bill that Kennedy got through the Congress, and it was partly because Secretary Hodges was willing to do the detail and congressional front running as well as carrying the ball."

Dr. Behrman thinks Hodges' travels helped not only trade relationships but contributed to the morale of Department of Commerce people stationed over the nation and around the world. "He visited the outposts, even the Antarctic expedition near the South Pole," said Behrman. It was at McMurdo Sound that Luther caught a fish by sinking a line 100 feet through the ice! "Hodges' presence there was useful," said Behrman. "It's good for the bosses to be seen around the diggings."

Behrman put a finger on another development under Hodges, one that has not proved its success yet—but may in the future. That is the development of the nuclear-powered steamship **N.S.S. Savannah**, a Maritime Administration try at saving shipping costs. The project is now abandoned, but it was a pioneering effort that may sometime in the future be revived.

These were achievements noted by his colleagues in Washington. As his staff members asserted, he was fatherly, sometimes a bit on the dutch uncle side. And he consistently admonished his staff members when they drove with him to "fasten your seat belts."

Approaching the age of 67, Luther Hodges spoke to President Johnson as early as October 1964, and suggested it was about time he should retire. Johnson urged him to delay his announcement. Then on December 16, 1964, LBJ acquiesced. He wrote to Luther Hodges:

I am personally reluctant to accept your resignation. Your achievements as Secretary of Commerce have been a continuation of selfless, patriotic dedication you have exhibited throughout your long service to your State and your Nation. Your leadership in the Commerce Department has been marked by prudence and progress.

President Johnson, below this typewritten message, inscribed in his own hand, "You have been aided by that wonderful American lady Martha." Mrs. Johnson held a farewell tea for Martha, and in January 1965, the Luther Hodges' headed for home in Chapel Hill.

The third week in January every year newspaper editors, publishers and prize winning reporters and editorial writers and correspondents assemble in

Chapel Hill at the annual North Carolina Press Institute. It is sponsored yearly by the University. In addition to the serious discussion of journalism, the University gives a luncheon for the press at which levity is the custom. On this occasion a quintet of newspapermen dressed like "The Beatles" sang songs. A "mystery guest" was also billed for the occasion. The secret guest, of course, was Luther Hodges. When the curtain was separated and the Press "Beatles" swung into music, the audience of some three hundred newspapermen saw Governor Hodges sitting there in a rocking chair and reading a newspaper. Emotional pandemonium reigned. All were on their feet in uproarious applause. It was obvious that North Carolinians were touched and delighted to have Luther Hodges back home again.

But Luther would have none of this mushy stuff. He stood and danced a modified version of the "twist" as the other newspapermen on the stage were doing, and followed this by a little speech saying how glad he and Martha were to be back with their home state friends.

Chapter Twenty

Luther Helps His Alma Mater

Luther became a dollar-a-year man for the North Carolina Research Triangle Foundation. He said with an amused smile, "I'll take the job on one condition: that I get paid in quarterly installments." Twenty-five cents every three months was a much lower wage than the five cents an hour he'd worked for, over fifty years before, in the textile mill at Spray. But laboring for the Research Triangle that he had helped to found—and selling North Carolina and its future to industrialists of the world—was like throwing Br'er Rabbit in the briar patch: Luther Hodges thrived on it. His title was Chairman of the Board of the Research Triangle Foundation, the organization that raises the money and makes the contacts between industry on the move and the Research Triangle. His offices are nine miles from Chapel Hill in the Hanes Building of the Triangle Park. He has an assistant and a clerical staff, all of them paid a hundred to a thousand times more than he is paid.

He accepted another part-time job, a lectureship in the School of Business Administration of the University in Chapel Hill. He speaks to classes in business several times a year, and invites questions about business and government. He teaches on movement of industry, organization of government, business and government interrelationships, how a large federal department is organized and how it operates. The reception to the Hodges lectures has been good, from the standpoints of the University, the students and Hodges. "They ask lots of questions," he said. "I'm impressed by the brightness of the students, their seriousness, their basically good character, the interest they have in communicating their thoughts. I like the new approaches they bring up."

That first January day following his return from Washington, Luther stood in the wings at the Carolina Inn ballroom stage in Chapel Hill. He was about to be welcomed back by the press of the state. It was an hour of fun. But there was a serious moment backstage when the subject of the University and the "Speaker Ban" was mentioned. His countenance became grave, and he said, "The University has a serious problem."

Indeed the University was in danger. Two years before, the 1963 General Assembly passed a "visiting speakers law." It forbade "known communists" from speaking on campuses of public colleges and universities of the state. Included in the ban were persons who had "taken the fifth" amendment to the U. S. Constitution in loyalty cases.

The law was passed in a sudden outburst, enacted on the last day the legislature convened. The normal rules were suspended, and the speaker of the house of representatives used what the newspapers called a "fast gavel." The newspapers and a large segment of the public raised an outcry. But the deed was done. It was too late to do anything about it The question was how serious the damage was to free speech and to academic freedom. Many contended that Chapel Hill's reputation as a free forum was at stake. Others wondered whether the regional accrediting body, the Southern Association of Colleges and Schools, might take some action. After protests the matter subsided for a time. A policy of watchful waiting prevailed. There was hope that the 1965 General Assembly would rescind the hasty action of the 1963 legislators.

Causes of the abrupt legislative action were easy to explain. The national ferment and unrest in the nation by racial minorities and their supporters in the Civil Rights movement had reached into North Carolina. Equal rights were demanded, especially in public accommodations such as restaurants, motels, places of assembly, buses and trains. Demonstrators marched. They carried picket signs. They sat-in. There were lie-ins and blocking of traffic. A center of the demonstrations was Chapel Hill. The demonstrators were several dozens of students and a few faculty members.

Chapel Hill and the whole University community have a mixed image in the public mind. It has traditionally been a place of controversy, of discussion, of liberal thought, of exploration leading to change, of free speech; often the university suffers the consequences of unbridled voicing of opinions; reprimands are strong, critical, moralistic. Chancellor Emeritus Robert B. House once said, "Chapel Hill is a place where some of the finest people in the world live, and where all hell is liable to break loose any minute." Louisville **Courier-Journal** publisher Mark Ethridge said in 1935, "Chapel Hill is the capital of the southern mind." It is a place of "small town living and cosmopolitan thinking," said Ward Allen Howe of **The Christian Science Monitor.** On his way home back to England after a year as a visiting professor in Chapel Hill, on Oxford scholar paced the deck of the **Queen Mary** and reflected on his experiences in the University of North Carolina. Then suddenly he was poetically inspired and he wrote this message back to a friend in the University, "Chapel Hill and its whole community is like a happy ship of folk, Franklin Street like its promenade deck, and walks in the village a series of meetings and pleasant greetings. But below the decks the great engines are at work."

That was the favorable view, the "Southern part of heaven" image. But during the 175 years of the University's history there have been those who projected an entirely different picture. Attitudes of faculty and students who take the activist line have been deplored over scores of years. Detractors who scrutinize the University under a different kind of microscope say "Chapel Hill is a cauldron of Communism." In 1799 a man wrote a letter to a North

Carolina editor: "A number of faculty have been found to be infidels, Catholics, anarchists and atheists." In 1865 a writer for the **Delphi Papers** said, "The university is a pestilential hotbed of slavocracy." Eruptions of criticism about communism at the University came in the 1930's, again in the early 1950's, and in a torrent in 1962 and 1963. There were many who declared that communists were very likely behind the Civil Rights movement. Chapel Hill as usual became the scapegoat community.

The University was weathering the criticism with its customary composure in 1963, taking a middle course, not interfering with the demonstrations, nor was it cooperating with them. Chapel Hill was playing its traditional role as a citadel of free speech and free peaceable assembly. As long as the students confined their actions to the campus and town of Chapel Hill there was little trouble. But then the pickets and demonstrators went to Raleigh where the General Assembly was in session! They paraded with signs in front of the Sir Walter Hotel where most of the assemblymen live during the legislative session. Legislators were antagonized! There were episodes of hot words between pickets and individual legislators.

House Bill 1395 was entitled "An Act to Regulate Visiting Speakers at State-Supported Colleges and Universities." It was passed.

The University and the trustees bided their time. There was hope that the 1965 Legislature would repeal the law. But as January 1965 came and the General Assembly prepared to meet there were those who threatened that the law would be made even stronger and Chapel Hill slapped harder—in appropriations and otherwise—if there were an attempt to alter the visiting speakers law. This was the reason for the whispered backstage comment by Luther Hodges at the Carolina Inn that the "university has a serious problem."

Governor Dan K. Moore appointed a blue ribbon commission to study the effects of the law and to report back later in the year, after the legislative session. Gov. Moore was criticized by a few for not opposing the law outright and for not vigorously seeking its repeal. But in retrospect, and in view of the final results, it is apparent that his judgment was correct.

The chairman of the Governor's Committee to study the Speaker Ban law was Senator David Britt. Britt had voted for the law but was considered a fair-minded man. He was a graduate of the Wake Forest College Law School. The other members of the commission were equally distinguished. Mr. Britt invited all who wished to be heard by his commission in open hearings at Raleigh on September 8-9, 1965. President William Friday of the University joined his chancellors and others in expressing the formal request by the trustees to **amend** the Speaker Ban law. Amendment would give authority back to the trustees, place it in the hands of chancellors who would establish "equal time" and open forums. Amendment, rather than repeal, would also help those in favor of the Speaker Ban law to react to compromise.

Speaking for a panel of University of North Carolina alumni were attorney Kemp D. Battle of Rocky Mount, Dr. Dewey Dorsett of Charlotte, Major L. P. McLendon of Greensboro, D. Edward Hudgins of Greensboro, Vermont C. Royster who is editor of the **Wall Street Journal**, James McMillan who is a Charlotte lawyer, former North Carolina attorney general Malcolm Seawell, and Samuel I. Parker of Concord, a retired chemical company executive.

The alumni committee, headed by attorney McMillan, had asked Governor Luther Hodges to appear on the panel with the other alumni. However, it was finally decided that Gov. Hodges would be more effective by speaking separately and as former governor of the state and Chairman of the Research Triangle Foundation.

Vermont C. Royster, a University of North Carolina graduate of 1935, said:

It is an unwise law enacted by good men with worthwhile intent. The law will not accomplish what it intends. That makes it a futile law. It will do a great many unintended injuries. That makes it a foolish law. And a law which is both futile and foolish is a bad law.

A ripple of applause, quickly hushed, broke out when Colonel Samuel I. Parker, a winner of the Congressional Medal of Honor for acts of heroism in World War I, came forward. Colonel Parker, a retired industrialist, said:

The Speaker Ban law is an insult to the intelligence, to the moral courage and stamina of young people of our state. I beg you to amend this law.

The other alumni speakers stressed the logic and the importance of amending the gag law. Those speaking for retention of the law were vigorous, too: Senator Robert Morgan; Colonel Henry Royall, a retired army man from Chapel Hill who said "you can just feel communism in the air at Chapel Hill" although he couldn't identify any individuals; representatives of the American Legion; John Wilkinson, a Republican leader from Washington, N. C., and others.

The Rev. B. Frank Hall, representing the Synod of the North Carolina Presbyterian Church, was heard. Hall was so persuasive that after he had completed his address, one of the Britt Commission members, attorney William T. Joyner of Raleigh said, "Dr. Hall, you are so persuasive that I am glad you are not a communist speaking on a platform in the university." Reverend Mr. Hall said:

> We believe that the only Christian, American and educationally effective way for free men to counter communism is by frank and honest confrontation. The way of concealment and repression of argument is the totalitarian way; the way of Stalin and Hitler . . . . To seek to muzzle one's opponents is to admit lack of faith in America . . . . In our opinion the Speaker Ban law is un-American . . . . The Spanish Inquisition had its origin in so simple a philosophy as the Speaker Ban law. It is always dangerous to proscribe. Nazism did this and the results are well-known.

Then David Britt called upon Luther Hodges. The **Under the Dome** column in the Raleigh **News and Observer** said the next day: "If facial expressions on the Speaker Ban Study Commission members can be taken as an accurate gauge, Luther Hodges made the greatest impact of any witness appearing before the Commission."

The former governor and former U. S. Secretary of Commerce said:

I am Luther H. Hodges of Chapel Hill, North Carolina, speaking as an individual citizen of our state . . . .

Within the last 60 days a prominent representative of a state competing with North Carolina (for new industry) said to me, "We will give you about two years before North Carolina begins to lose its leadership in securing strong support from industry and government" . . . .

My premise is that damage can come to our educational institutions and to our good state . . . . we must try to be calm and practical in these trying times . . . . I would sincerely and earnestly urge that both sides in this controversy give a little for the sake of the state.

Luther Hodges was speaking frankly for compromise. His words, and the words of others before the Britt Commission, were heeded. The Britt group recommended amendment of the Speaker Ban Law, which was what the University had requested. Governor Dan Moore called the special session of the Legislature. There was a new skirmish and a new debate. By this time the Governor and David Britt led the way for the University.

The special and extraordinary session of the General Assembly amended the Speaker Ban law, returning to the institutions the authority to regulate visiting speakers.

An onus was off the University's back. A restriction on freedom of speech was removed. But there was another gratifying byproduct. For years, the university has been sniped at by those alleging "communism." President William Friday said he knew of no communists and if there were any who could name communists in the University to do so. No names were brought forth. David Britt in his report to Governor Moore gave the University a clean bill of health on the matter of excessive liberalism, communism, leftist leanings. The canards of over a century cannot be removed all at once. However, when a reckless accuser of the future shouts "communism" at the University of North Carolina, an historic document that was produced after a thorough investigation by a Blue Ribbon Governor's Commission in 1965 can be offered in refutation. The Britt Commission stated:

> The evidence before this commission failed to disclose that the faculty of the University at Chapel Hill is infiltrated by Communists. The evidence shows that the university does not foster nor encourage any political doctrine that would suppress the liberty or freedom of any individual.

> We believe that it is highly desirable that students have the opportunity to question, review and discuss the opinions of speakers representing a wide range of viewpoints. It is vital to our success in supporting our free society against all forms of totalitarianism that institu-

tions remain free to examine these ideologies in a manner consistent with educational objectives.

The evidence before us fails to justify charges of irresponsible radicalism at Chapel Hill.

The University of North Carolina at Chapel Hill is a great institution that has served the state well. Members of the General Assembly and all citizens of our state are justifiably interested in our university. There is no evidence of plot, plan, campaign, or conspiracy by anyone to injure the university or any state-supported college.

One of the speakers who banned the speaker ban was U.N.C. Class of 1919 graduate, Marshall Field executive, North Carolina Governor and United States Commerce Department Secretary Luther H. Hodges, who spoke effectively for his alma mater and for freedom of speech.

Incoming and outgoing Rotary International Presidents at Spring meeting in Chapel Hill in 1967. Luther H. Hodges, left, Richard Evans, right.

Chapter Twenty-one

"He Profits Most Who Serves Best"

One winter evening early in 1966 Luther Hodges was visiting in New York City. "I was out on the town," said Luther, which means that he was seeing a Broadway show. He was late getting back to the hotel that night, about 11:30, and a telephone call was waiting.

"We have been meeting all day," said the chairman of a Rotary committee, "going over names of Rotarians who have been supported as a possible president of Rotary International. I am authorized by the committee to say that you are our choice. You're it, if you'll take it."

The presidency of Rotary International is not a job that one runs for. It is not sought as one seeks a political office. Luther Hodges knew that his name had been mentioned several times over the years for the top post in Rotary, and he had made up his mind that if he were tapped for the presidency he would say yes. A founder of the Leaksville club in 1923, district governor in North Carolina, President of the

New York City club, chairman of important international committees and a director, Luther had lived the principles of Rotary. Outside his family and his work, Rotary was first. Indeed, Rotary had been a part of his work and the life of his family. Often when he addressed church congregations, his text was as likely to be taken from Rotary ideals as from the Bible.

Two Rotary slogans are: "Service above Self" and "He Profits Most Who Serves Best." Luther Hodges has lived those precepts from his boyhood. Serving others was Luther's watchword from the time he swept the floor of his father's grocery store; from the day the executives of the Leaksville mill first said, "Let Luther do it;" from the hard work and service to his fellow students at Chapel Hill; from the decisions reflecting personal integrity and leadership when he was governor of North Carolina; from his international perceptions of free interchange of ideas and goods and his service as Secretary of Commerce and for which President Lyndon B. Johnson lauded Hodges for his "selfless" service. Luther Hodges had "served best." He also had profited—and others had profited because he had profited and he had served.

Before his installation as President at the Nice convention in July, 1967, Luther expressed a four-point "call to action" to Rotarians all over the world. To the 12,803 Rotary Clubs and 613,500 Rotarians in 134 countries at that time Luther addressed a message: "Let"s Make Our Rotary Membership Effective."

In his own words, this is the way he proposed to do it:

First: Get personally involved in Rotary. Rotary must, of course, be modern in its approach to the complicated problems of today's world, but its basic approach must remain simple. Flexibility goes hand in hand with Rotary. So long as Rotary is experienced as a simple appeal to the heart for comradeship in service to others, it can move men to great endeavor . . . .

Second: Exercise leadership by being successful in your business or profession. There is so much talk these days about success being a siren which lures men into a ruthless disregard for the interests and rights of others. This is mostly nonsense. Most business and professional men are ethical and considerate, but there is a minority which gives us trouble. I believe that the **first** job of a Rotarian is to be successful in his business or profession and in his family life . . . .

Third: Be loyal to your community and nation and serve them whenever possible. Whatever the circumstances of your community, you can exercise leadership by maintaining your pride in it. Loyalty to the future can be productive and creative. Loyalty recognizes the needs, the failings, and the problems of the community as **opportunities.**

Fourth: Keep informed and develop an understanding of the problems of peoples of other nations. The best world citizen is that citizen who is both proud of and loyal to his own community and nation in the spirit I have previously described. The contribution he makes to the improvement of his own community is a substantial addition to world progress. Still, he needs to be informed on affairs of the world community. The world fellowship of Rotary in 134 countries offers an incomparable resource of first-hand information. I hope that increasingly what we call "World Community Service" will translate into personal service abroad by Rotarians who have retired. The experience of a lifetime can often be extremely helpful in helping people of developing countries to help themselves.

In his final emphasis Luther challenged his fellow Rotarians to become international-minded, and to do so by first being local-minded. His hope that retired Rotarians who have something to offer in aiding those in underdeveloped nations was immediately adopted as a 1967-68 Rotary program over the world. "Rotary Volunteers Abroad" is the name of the project.

The plan works like this: A retired Rotarian who has the vigor to give others the benefit of his counsel volunteers to go to some other nation and aids in some business, industrial, education, public service or other approved project. All is arranged through Rotary—in the sending country where the retired executive comes from and in the receiving country where the task is to be performed. It is financed both by Rotary International and by each nation obtaining the assistance. Rotary International pays the fare of the retired Rotarian and his wife to and from the foreign country. Their expenses in the country accepting the benefits are paid at that end. By the first part of 1968 Luther was able to disclose that eight or nine retired Rotarians had been lined up—with matching receptivity for useful "service above self."

Simultaneously Luther moved to build up Rotary at the grassroots. He set in motion a world-wide series of meetings called the "District Leadership Forum;" teams of Rotarians and individuals traveled at their own expense to talk with other Rotary Clubs within the district—**to talk Rotary.**

"Talking Rotary" means discussion of what **other** clubs are doing, what clubs can be doing better, and what Rotary means "in practical terms," said Luther. His purpose was to strengthen the membership—and to start new clubs. To set the example, his hometown club in Chapel Hill sponsored the formation of a second club in the University of North Carolina community. Rotary established "leadership forums" available to each district, and named 61 past officers of Rotary International to serve as moderators of the forums. The new program, said Luther to his fellow Rotarians, "will be a great step in filling what I have called a Rotary information gap." Luther Hodges was applying to Rotary International the same principles of self-examination, firm organization at the foundation, and internal communication that had characterized his organizational improvements in business and government.

He gave attention to the central Rotary offices and the staff and services rendered. This included establishing a full-fledged public relations department of Rotary at the offices in Evanston, Illinois. This is in addition to the news office and the excellent magazine, **The Rotarian.** A new staff was hired to inaugurate a general communications and public relations program by contacts with mass and special media.

In **The Rotarian**, President Luther gave short messages from time to time to the hundreds of thousands of Rotarians over the world. For instance, in the December 1967 edition, he plugged better programs for Rotary meetings. He asked these questions: "Is your club program informative? . . . . Is it effectively run—on time? . . . . Is the program challenging?"

He traveled. Traveling isn't unusual for Luther Hodges, but one 5-week's trip to 20 countries of Africa may be considered one highlight of his Rotary administration. Trip Letters sent back to family and friends focus a staccato kaleidoscope of the Rotary Clubs on the continent of Africa. Accompanying Hodges was Leroy Williams of Swainsboro, Georgia. Williams is a former first vice-president of Rotary International.

Foresighted Luther Hodges arranged his "affairs in order" before he left Chapel Hill in late October. Luther is not fatalistic. Rather he inclines to optimism. But he is prudent, so on the outside chance he might not make it back to the United States, his will and kindred necessary documents were brought up to date. Another precaution was taken: Luther packed 30 boxes of corn flakes and other dry cereal. Whenever he travels abroad and questions the food at some particular place, he takes no chances. He likes foreign and exotic foods and seeks them out.

But he also is cautious, and if it seems risky, he politely turns down the food, and eats his own corn-flakes or bran. At one stop on the African journey, he was not able to get the kind of milk he wanted so he ate his emergency cornflakes with soda water. At other times he feasted on rare viands. The consequence was that Luther remained in the best of health all during the five weeks of hopping from nation to nation by plane.

Their first African visit was in Sierra Leone. No other Rotary president has visited the "Lion Mountains," a melting pot for freed slaves. Luther addressed the Freetown Rotary Club, and heard reports on their projects, including aid in maternity and mental hospitals.

Their plane flight from Freetown to the Ivory Coast cancelled, the Rotary twosome chartered a special plane and flew to Abijan. Abijan is known as the "Paris of West Africa." Luther wrote the log of his visits, from the Ivory Coast to Dahomey in the country of Cotonou, and thence to Gabon, Cameroun, the Central African Republic, Nigeria, Niger, Ghana, South West Africa, Swaziland and Mozambique. They flew to Mauritius, Reunion, and Madagascar and on to Comoro Islands, Tanzania, Uganda, Rwanda, and Burundi. Hodges and Williams usually stayed at hotels, but sometimes found it more convenient to accept the hospitality of local Rotary clubs. They were greeted at airports and spoke at Rotary luncheons and dinners.

At Abijan as elsewhere, Luther challenged the Rotary Club to send one or more Rotarians to the

1968 international convention at Mexico City, and to "send us a project for Rotary Volunteers Abroad." The Cotonou Rotary Club showed the visitors through a tuberculosis wing at a local hospital given by the club.

At the town of Ganvie—sometimes called the Village on Stilts, Leroy Williams and Luther Hodges found a slight language difficulty that was quite amusing. The French-speaking natives referred to Leroy in the French manner—**le roi,** for king. "They had billed me as Martin Luther Hodges," wrote Luther, "but now they have it correct."

Luther presented to the president of the country some tiny brick cuff links. The cuff links are symbols of North Carolina's progress and tell a little story. He has a quantity of the brick cuff links and gives them with the message of the Tar Heel State. The story: a man in a bleak, red-clay section of North Carolina wondered what he could do to make a living on the eroded countryside. Finally he started a brick-yard, utilizing the clay, and he made money.

At Windhoek, South West Africa, they visited an "old service Rotarian confined to his house with a heart attack." At Bangui, the Central African Republic, Luther wrote:

> Most of the 30 members of the Bangui Rotary Club met us and that evening had a ladies night meeting at the new Safari Hotel. Here was an affair—beautifully gowned women (some with mini-skirts) a gourmet dinner featuring the best-cooked quail I've tasted, champagne and wines flowing (It took three hours to serve the meal) . . . .

At Saint-Denis in the nation of Reunion, Luther planted a "tree of friendship" in memory of President John F. Kennedy. At one French-speaking place, Luther remarked that he'd better go over the two or three jokes he tells, so that the French translator will "insure getting the French punch line in the proper place and with the proper emphasis."

After flying from Zanzibar to Entebbe-Kampala, Uganda, Williams and Hodges had a good night's sleep. He writes:

I awakened this Monday morning to the sound of roosters crowing, ducks quacking, and dogs barking. Reminded me of my boyhood home in Leaksville where all those things were then taken for granted . . . . except that I was now in a 16-story, 600 room, $12 million hotel owned by the Uganda government . . . . As always, we asked to see the market and find out what the people sold and ate. I bought some small, sweet bananas at a penny each and saw some "passion fruit" but decided I didn't need any . . . . At the dinner where I spoke there were 250 present, including men and women from Kampala and two other clubs in Uganda. Reception and dinner went from 6:30 to 11 p.m. Many of the leading Rotarians complained how poor their clubs were, that they needed help. Yet at the dinner they raffled off a ticket for a small prize with a first bid of 5 pounds ($2.80 a pound) and a final bid of 105 pounds.

Our plane was over two hours late getting to Addis Ababa, Ethiopia from Nairobi in Kenya . . . . Ethiopia is one of the most interesting of all the places. Had a television interview this morning and another this afternoon. They asked me to tell about Rotary. We got in some of the projects of the local club, such as artificial limbs for the handicapped, braille typewriters for the blind . . . . The whole Rotary Club met us at the Djibouti airport . . . . Malta was our last stop and was a delightful place to close our tour of Rotary countries and clubs . . . . It has been a great trip! We spoke to 22 Rotary Clubs in 20 countries and touched down in 28 countries . . . . we covered 29,304 miles—not a date broken and not a bag delayed . . . . Rotary is strong and growing. It is well embraced and well received in these countries. Our decision to visit the small clubs will pay off.

In his reading habits, Luther Hodges delves into biography. He's a mystery story reader, too. He leans much of the time to books on the history of world religions. He is interested in the teachings of Christ, Moses, Mohammed and Buddha. The ideals they hold up he sees reflected in an idea called Rotary, and Rotary he practices with a quiet fervor. Rotary provides him the inspiration that goes with public service and furnishes for him the balancing column for the other two pillars of his personal architectural structure—his day-to-day professional life and his devotion to his family. The presidency of Rotary International is a labor of affection for an organization he loves.

A man of medium height, five feet and eleven inches, and well-proportioned frame that is only a few pounds over his weight when he played basketball in Chapel Hill half a century ago, Luther Hodges has a handsome, masculinely-rugged face. His smile is ready and his expression can change rapidly dependent upon his alert change of pace as one bit of information after another captures his attention. He doesn't have a poker face—he registers his feelings —but there is no great extreme of reactions on his countenance, or actions. He is a man of moderation, pleasant, yet intense, restless, driving, impatient. But the impatience is creative impatience. His motivations are positive. He strives to leave things better than they were before. He speaks in a well-modulated baritone, pleasing to the ear, distinctly and articulately, though a trifle fast. In presiding over the world's most far-flung civic organization, this man of creative impatience, always willing to take charge in an emergency, possessing the go-go tendencies of the modern generation while clinging to ancient moral precepts, including his business and political life, is devoting to the Rotary International presidency the same skills and dynamism that has energized all institutions with which he has been associated.

Secretary of Commerce Luther H. Hodges holds airport press conference on arrival in Seoul, Korea, Nov. 9, 1962. He was on a month-long, round the world trip to spur two-way trade, tourism and foreign investment.

Chapter Twenty-two

A Task-Oriented Man

If you said that the presidency of Rotary International is the final crowning public enterprise of Luther Hodges' career, it would be a risky and unlikely assumption. He would probably confound the prophet and take on some other big job. When he does complete his Rotary year, he expects to return to Chapel Hill and concentrate on his personal business affairs. This includes membership on the board of directors of six national and international financial-industrial organizations. He will lecture occasionally in the university and keep up his industry-hunting for North Carolina through the Research Triangle Foundation, and there will be special public service projects, including higher education counseling. One anniversary that's impending is the 50th reunion of the University of North Carolina class of 1919, to be held in Chapel Hill in June, 1969.

His business interests to which he will devote his attention are Drexel Enterprises of Morganton, N. C., including furniture manufacturing; Williams

Brothers Great Lakes Pipeline; the Gulf & Western Board of New York, a conglomerate of corporations; the Glen Alden Corporation of New York (Paul Johnston is president of the firm); Servomation, a vending machine concern; Financial Consultants International, mutual investments fund organization operating abroad but not in the United States. He is chairman of the board of the latter organization.

His daily agenda probably won't change much. Martha and Luther keep in touch with their friends. Betsy Hodges Bernard and her family pop into Chapel Hill frequently from Short Hills, New Jersey on many occasions, and Nancy Hodges Finlay and her family try to come from India at least once a year. Luther H. Hodges Jr. is senior vice-president of the North Carolina National Bank in the state. Luther Jr. is also writing a book on industrial investments and is Chairman of Gov. Dan K. Moore's Manpower Commission for the state, a cooperative effort between government and industry to retrain men and women in skills and promote employment. Asked by a reporter whether he was interested in politics and being governor of North Carolina, Luther Hodges Jr. says "maybe later." He added: "It's good business to be involved in politics. The problem is you can't take time out from the business world. There are a lot of segments of our society who think the job is over at 5 o'clock. If it is, we're in trouble. Somebody will step in to fill the vacuum." The similarity of what the two Hodges', father and son, might say under similar circumstances is striking.

When the juggling acts of his personal businesses, North Carolina's problems and the extra civic chores he's assumed exert too much pressure upon him, Luther Hodges Sr. will take off for a mountain stream or an ocean trawler and he will drop a line in the water and achieve the tranquility that derives from the primeval activity of catching a fish. There is always the likelihood, too, that some fire will break out, some emergency in government or education in North Carolina, that will invite his attention and his moderating judgment, just as he helped to save the day in the Speaker Ban controversy.

Luther Hodges is a man of complex personality. It is not reasonable to say to a boy or a young man: follow in his footsteps and you will achieve success. For times change, and what may contribute to the success of one man may not suffice in the case of another. Yet it is proper that young people who try to find the "secret" to the kind of success achieved by Luther Hodges be told of the life of this remarkable man. For Luther Hodges is a classical Horatio Alger type of the 20th century. He was a poor boy who has achieved his goals and is living The American Dream. Luther Hodges will be the first to say there is no "secret formula" for success. The mystery is too deep; no simple combination of numbers can be turned to unlock the safe in which will be found valuable information edifying to those who would follow a path similar to that traveled by Luther Hodges.

However, it is worth reaffirming some of the ideals and the accomplishments of a boy who rose

by his own bootstraps. The example could be profit-
able to many who heed the story.

Psychologists who study human behavior list
people into two classifications: **One**, those who are
peer-oriented, and **two**, those who are task-oriented.
People who are oriented to tasks live by a code of
conduct, a strict set of ethical rules. These rules
furnish a yardstick for measuring what is right and
wrong. A judge on the bench follows such rules.
Justice is blind, or it should be. A judge should not
favor a man before the bar because that man is a
friend or a relative, or because he is black or white.
A priest or a minister is also task-oriented, and so
are other kinds of professional and businessmen, including the best newspaper editors. On the other
hand, those who are oriented by association with
their fellows, or their peers, to conforming to what
others think, or to the sway of public opinion, right
or wrong, are peer-oriented. Psychologists find that
teen-agers and other young people are peer-oriented.
They find it difficult to take a stand independent of
the opinions and pressures of their associates and
professional colleagues. As they mature, they are
able to resist the pressures of the crowd, to throw
off the shackles of conformity, and to live by principle, by ethical standards, by a code of conduct.
Perhaps that is one sign of maturity—the degree to
which one is able to live as a Man of Principle. Most
people sometimes follow both the rules and the in-
fluences exerted by their peers. When there are conflicts of interests they have to choose between principle and the regard of their associates or colleagues
or age group, or family or fraternity or race. The

most mature individuals live by rules and become the nation's leaders.

It appears that Luther Hodges achieved a high degree of maturity early in life. In part, it was forced on him by adversity, by the harsh realities of his boyhood. There was in him also some inborn characteristic or instinct plus native intelligence. Added to that was encouragement that came to him by perceptive teachers. He was taught, and he believed, the tenets of the Christian religion. He was subjected to discipline, and he was able to discipline himself. He became proficient in disciplining others. He was able to practice the art of renunciation, of biding his time, doing the dirty work; later, the rewards poured in. He was bookish, but he was extrovertish, too. His attitude was strict and stern, but moderated with a soft voice, a smiling mein, an understanding heart. There is no doubt that he is a striking example of the task-oriented man.

If a few simple rules of behavior were to be stated as the essence of his character, perhaps these would be appropriate:

1. Be honest, truthful, straight-forward.
2. Be on time. Punctuality is a virtue.
3. Work. Even take on the dirty tasks. Do more than your part.
4. Find ways to do the job better. Insist on quality performance. Avoid waste. Be accurate and complete. Toe the line, and insist that others do the same.
5. Educate yourself. Strive for excellence in studies. Don't settle for second best. Be an A-

student, a 100 percent perfect scholar as far as you possibly can.

6. Ask questions of your fellows. Learn from them. When you meet a man with a special skill, ask him to teach you, to tell you how he does it.

7. Don't be altogether a drudge. Play. Take part in athletics. Be competitive. Learn to speak, to debate, to assume leadership, to perform public service. Be versatile, well-rounded.

8. Avoid nepotism in business. Strictly avoid favoring friends or relatives in public jobs or in business.

9. When you do a personal favor for a relative or friend, do it privately, even secretly.

10. Live daily by the precepts of the Golden Rule and the Ten Commandments and the other teachings of Jesus Christ. Pray.

11. Organize your time, budget your hours and minutes, make each moment count. Learn to grasp facts quickly, cut away the froth.

12. Set priorities on your time and interests. Choose the most important things to do first, and concentrate on these.

13. Select your career and your civic opportunities with care.

14. Set long-range goals. Study the tasks. Master the job. Then handle the details day by day. Assemble the facts, weigh them, make decisions as soon as you can do so with justice to the task.

15. When you have reached a position of authority and control the activities of many people, learn to delegate authority. Follow up to see that the many subdivisions of jobs are done.

16. Be strict in demanding quality performance,

even to the point of impatience. Don't put up with shoddy work. Be hard-nosed. Eschew chit-chat and foolishness during business hours. Be tough; not ugly tough, but tough.

17. Communicate in plain language. Don't be misunderstood. Be sure your instructions are complete. Get a feedback. Require reports and results.

18. Keep up your contacts with friends and acquaintances.

19. Be a good salesman. Make a good product. Believe in your product. Talk about your product. Advertise it. Boost it. Sell it. Make a profit.

20. Recognize there are more than one or two ways to achieve an objective. If the first attempt does not pay off, try another approach. This is a variation on the old familiar theme of "there's more than one way to skin a cat" and "if at first you don't succeed, try, try again." The main thing to remember is that in trying again and again, don't assume you should try doing it the identical way you tried the last time. Go at it from another angle. Be resourceful and persistent.

21. Be brief. Cut out the fluff in business conversation. Focus on the lean, muscular facts.

22. Surround yourself with creative people. Take their ideas, and select the ones that will work.

23. Have faith in education and especially in research. Explore new ideas. Find new ways of doing things.

24. Don't be an extremist. Be moderate. Don't lose your temper. Don't make a scene.

25. Protect your health. Take exercise. Don't get flabby. Eat carefully. Go to bed at a reasonable

hour, get plenty of sleep. Go to a doctor who practices preventive medicine and keeps you well.

26. Have trust in free institutions, free speech, academic freedom. Protect and defend these freedoms.

27. Practice confidence in the free enterprise system. At the same time insist on high ethical principles in trade, fair income for labor, fairness in price and just treatment of the customer.

28. Be independent. Don't be obligated or "beholden." Pay your debts.

29. Keep busy. Drive. Stay on the ball, even to the extent of being tight as a G-string.

30. Understand power and influence and traditions of the press, and cooperate in communicating with the people.

31. Have the moral strength to be indignant on proper provocation, but don't lose your poise.

32. Remember that service comes before self.

33. Learn the art of renunciation; that is, give up transient joys of the present for more lasting rewards to be gained later.

34. Use adversity to good advantage. Profit by mistakes, yours and others.

35. Know how to say "no," kindly, smilingly, firmly, definitely.

36. Cling to high ideals.

37. Don't make a fuss about trivial matters that can't be avoided or retrieved; but attend to the little details; be thoughtful and maintain contacts.

38. When onerous, difficult, necessary work has to be done, do it cheerfully.

39. Try the new. Sample new food, new people, new ideas, exotic and cosmopolitan places. But cling to the simple, the tried and true, the fundamental virtues. Turnip greens, hashed brown potatoes, corn bread, persimmon pudding, black-eyed peas, buttermilk.

These are rough rules that reflect the life a complex man, a mysterious individual, who lives by a number of simple but rigid rules. A sophisticated man of volcanic energy and finely-honed personal integrity, Luther Hodges is a supersalesman with a genuine missionary zeal to elevate standards for the good of the lives of his fellow men.